**W9-BTO-957**

THE MILITIA MOVEMENT

Fighters of the Far Right

THE MILITIA MOVEMENT

Fighters of the Far Right

BY BEN SONDER

Franklin Watts
A Division of Grolier Publishing
New York / London / Hong Kong / Sydney
Danbury, Connecticut

Cover illustration by Janet Hamlin.

Photographs ©: AP/Wide World Photos: 76 (John Flesher), 45 (Jeff T. Green), 14 (Bill Haber), 36 (Gary Stewart), 4 top, 27, 47, 64; Archive Photos: 87 (Jim Bourg/Reuters), 4 bottom; Corbis-Bettmann: 89 (Agence France Presse), 31, 53 (Reuters), 59, 66 (UPI); Globe Photos: 28 (Harris & Ewing); Jim West: 17; Liaison Agency, Inc.: 85 bottom (J. Pat Carter), 72 (R. "Chip" Ellis), 85 top (Fema), 6, 23, 26, 48 (Hulton Getty), 42 (Brad Markel), 104 (Tim Revel/Columbus Dispatch), 109 (William R. Sallaz), 61 (William Schaefer), 44 (James Woodcock), 98; Mark L. Wright: 8; Richard B. Levine: 10.

Visit Franklin Watts on the Internet at:
http://publishing.grolier.com

Library of Congress Cataloguing-in-Publication Data

Sonder, Ben. 1954-
The militia movement: fighters of the far right / by Ben Sonder.
p. cm.
Includes bibliographical references.
Summary: Discusses the history and philosophies of the far-right militia movement and its connections with hate groups and domestic terrorism.
   ISBN 0-531-11405-8 (lib. bdg.)   0-531-16466-7 (pbk)
   1. Militia movements–United States. 2. Terrorism–United States.
3. Government, Resistance to–United States. 4. Hate groups–United States.
5. Right-wing extremists–United States. [1. Militia movements. 2. Right-wing extremists. 3. Government, Resistance to. 4. Terrorism.] I. Title.
   HV6432.S69 2000
   322.4–2–0973–dc21
                                                        99-20321
                                                        CIP
                                                        AC

C O N T E N T S

Outlaw brothers Jesse (above)
and Frank James became icons
of Southern anger with
the United States
government during
the reconstruction era.

THE MILITIA MENTALITY

He was a God-fearing man from Missouri with mild blue eyes and small, delicate white hands. He was, in fact, the son of a Baptist minister. Those who knew him on a day-to-day basis were impressed by his good manners and his family values. But in 1882, a young recruit staying with him and his family shot him in the back of the neck. When news of the murder arrived at the Missouri state capitol, the governor breathed a sigh of relief: Jesse James, the notorious outlaw, was dead. His career as a bank and train robber was over.

There were a good number of Missourians who didn't share the governor's sentiment. They mourned Jesse James as if he had been a saint, a kind of Robin Hood who stole from the rich to give to the poor. Most of these people had supported the Confederacy during the Civil War, although officially Missouri had remained in the Union. Antislavery factions with connections to the industrial North had forcibly kept the state from seceding, but they had been bitterly opposed by groups of Confederate guerrillas in Missouri. One of the most notorious of these small armies was the Quantrill band, which killed more than 150 unarmed men, women, and children in the town of Lawrence, Kansas, in an attempt to advance the Confederate cause.

Jesse James and his older brother, Frank, were members of Quantrill's band and staunch supporters of the Confederate cause. Most of the brothers' violent acts before and during the Civil War were in the name of the Confederacy, but after the Civil War the James brothers'

7

On August 21, 1863, William Quantrill, the James brothers, and several other men killed 150 unarmed civilians in Lawrence, Kansas. The gang considered the townspeople to be Northern sympathizers.

actions became more ambiguous. The two men felt bitterness and resentment about the Northern victory, and, like some other rural Southerners, complained that the outcome of the Civil War had condemned them to powerlessness and poverty. Consequently, they hated the federal government, its laws, Northern businesses, and the control these powers had over the entire country.

Between 1866 and 1882, the James brothers and other former Quantrill raiders robbed banks, stagecoaches, and trains carrying gold. To most people, the bank robberies amounted to stealing the savings of ordinary citizens; but seizing gold had a much different image for some. Gold was associated with wealthy capitalists who, in the eyes of the James brothers and some other rural people, ran the country as tyrants. Gold represented the huge profits of the industrial North. It had little to do with the subsistence life of Missouri farmers, especially those living in the Ozarks who didn't care much about life outside the mountains and weren't very concerned about national politics. These were the people who were most likely to see the James brothers as heroes.

Although Jesse and his brother may or may have not shared the spoils of their thievery with their rural neighbors, a legend built up around them. Their lawlessness stood as a symbol of the hostility that certain people felt toward mainstream American politics and economics. In this way, both the James brothers and those who sympathized with them resembled some of the members of today's most extreme militias. These people also resent mainstream American politics. Many of them feel that the American economic and political system has left them stranded, with uncertain futures. Like the James brothers, they are willing, in some cases, to defy the laws of this country to achieve their ends.

What Is the American Militia Movement?

Officially, a militia is a part of the organized armed forces of a country that, unlike a standing army, is called upon only in an emergency. However, the militias that will be discussed in this book are unofficial citizens' armies organized by private individuals, usually with antigovernment, far-right agendas. This phenomenon is relatively recent. Although some of the attitudes, activities, and leaders that now give the militia movement force have existed in this country for decades—even farther back than Jesse James—most experts

9

The Southern Poverty Law Center in Montgomery, Alabama, is home to the nation's largest militia watchdog project. The Peace Memorial, located at the entrance to the center, was designed by artist Maya Lin and commemorates key events in the civil rights movement of the 1960s.

date the existence of the contemporary militia movement to the mid-1990s. There have been paramilitary groups with revolutionary ideas throughout America's history, but today's militia movement is a new, more organized, and more violent presence.

According to the Southern Poverty Law Center, an organization in Montgomery, Alabama, that monitors and takes legal action against the more dangerous militias, there were about 171 militia—meaning paramilitary—groups in the United States in 1998.[1] Most of these "citizen armies" have few members and are not involved in violent activities. They are interested merely in the purchase and use of firearms, in discussions of patriotism, and in playing weekend war games. However, more than a hundred of these groups probably have ties to violent right-wing and racist organizations.

10

This book will focus on these groups. It will also give information about the larger "Patriot" movement, which encompasses a variety of ultra-right-wing, often fanatically religious organizations, including militias, "common-law" courts, and other groups that provide information, tracts, videos, and ideas to the militias.

Unfortunately, the information provided by the Southern Poverty Law Center and other watchdog groups about the dangerous fringe of the militia world is sketchy. Much of it comes from informants and therefore can't easily be documented. The most dangerous margins of the Patriot movement are evasive and secretive. The groups they belong to may be little more than coalitions with loose, informal connections to one another. They are united not so much by bureaucratic structure as by a set of similar beliefs. Most of them are disenchanted with mainstream politics and the federal government and feel that only the most extreme, violent measures can change things. They oppose some basic laws now existing in this country as well as some of the later amendments to the Constitution. Some see violent disobedience as not only their right, but their duty.

Although most right-wing militia groups are not highly organized in the bureaucratic sense, their members sometimes work together in small groups to try to achieve their goals. These groups may stockpile weapons and military gear; train regularly for defensive and offensive war; engage in sporadic acts of violence against their enemies in government, law enforcement, and the media; write leaflets and create Web pages to spread their ideas; and meet to discuss strategies. The most recent method of organizing militia activities is in very tiny, underground groups of two to ten people known as "cells." Each cell has only limited knowledge of what the other is doing. That way, if one

Many militias and other extremist organizations disseminate information over the Internet.

underground cell is discovered or if a member becomes an informer, the others are not likely to be found out or harmed.

Portrait of a "Super-Patriot"

In the 1980s, more than a hundred years after Jesse James was killed, a man named Gordon Kahl also became a top-priority fugitive.[2] Kahl was a racist, anti-Semitic firearms activist who believed that the United States belonged only to white Christians. He was a member of the Posse Comitatus, a name which comes from the Latin for "power of the county." The Posse Comitatus had no central headquarters, no leader, and no constitution. It was a network of friends and acquaintances active during the 1970s and 1980s in the upper midwestern and western states. Members believed that federal and state law have no power and that the county sheriff, as long as he or she follows the will of the people, is the highest legitimate government authority.

In bold defiance of the federal government, Kahl refused to pay taxes. As a result, a U.S. marshal came to arrest him. After a 1983 shootout in North Dakota left a U.S. marshal and his deputy dead and three other law officers and Kahl's son wounded, Kahl escaped. During the five months that U.S. law enforcers looked for him, he became a hero among some people in the Dakotas, Arkansas, and other states. Many who knew where he was hiding refused to turn him in. They identified with his politics and praised him for so boldly defying the government. As had happened in the case of Jesse James, the law finally caught up with Kahl. In the course of another shootout, he was killed. But a month later, white supremacist leaders throughout the nation canonized him as the "first martyr of the Second American Revolution." Kahl is one of the "forefathers" of today's militia movement.

Private Armies

The most right-wing fringe members of the militia movement generally feel that the federal government is interfering with their "God-given" rights. To combat this government, they promote not only the ideal of individual resistance like Kahl's but also the ideal of citizen armies. They got the idea of a citizen army from a concept forged shortly after the Revolutionary War, when American colonists had just thrown off the tyrannical yoke of British government. When these colonists created the U.S. Constitution, they made a provision for the right of citizens to bear arms and for states to organize their own part-time armies, or militias. This provision is stated in the Second Amendment to the Constitution. Its purpose was partly to prevent any future central government from having too much power.

Militia groups today feel that the central government does have too much power and that the small, private armies they are organizing are merely versions of the state militias guaranteed by the Second Amendment. However, the Supreme Court has interpreted "militia" to mean a state-run army—the National Guard. Some militia members claim that these official armies are merely tools of the federal government. They believe that in certain situations, their citizen armies have the right to take the law into their own hands.

Conspiracy Theories and the Militia Movement

Most members of militias fear that a "New World Order" is coming in which the United States will be ruled by a dictatorship composed of government and corporate elites across the globe. With very little evidence, they formulated a theory that the nation's banks, federal government, courts, and large businesses are controlled by a small group of sinister, ruthless leaders, who meet in secret and whose power center is in the northern cities, especially in Washington, D.C. They fear that the federal government and big business are about to take away their basic freedoms, and they are obsessed with combating both of these forces by any means. The belief in national and worldwide conspiracies to undermine individual freedom is a basic tenet of extremist, far-right militias. In most cases, there is little or no hard evidence for these claimed conspiracies, but that doesn't stop ideas about them from proliferating.

Many right-wing militia members also think that the United Nations is a threat to American individualism. They say that its hidden objective is to enslave the world under one global, totalitarian government and that the United States should pull out of the United Nations immediately. They think that all of the activities of the federal government

14

are being secretly controlled by the United Nations and that the national media is cooperating with the United Nations to keep this information hidden.

In general, most members of militias want to force history backward, away from its current movement toward international cooperation and commerce and back to a time when small communities of people and individual initiative were what counted. Because of this, some militia members go so far as to claim that it is unwholesome for the United States to participate at all in world affairs. Many come close to wanting our country's foreign policy abolished entirely.

Racism and the Militia

A good share of right-wing militia and other Patriot groups promote racist and anti-Semitic ideas. They share a paranoid delusion that the country is under the power of a secret Jewish elite composed of bankers and business people who are supported by advocates of black power, feminism, and gay rights. Some militia members refer to the United States government as ZOG, or the Zionist Occupation Government, because they believe that certain high-profile Jews, along with others they imagine in the background, pull the strings of government. Some also believe that the country is threatened by armies composed of black and Latino street gangs, which are being secretly prepared by the federal government to take over the country.

Others claim that the only real citizens of the United States are white Christians and that Jews, blacks, and members of other ethnic groups do not belong in this country at all. Members of militias, Patriot groups, and far-right racist organizations have distributed documents detailing their elaborate plans for dividing the country into ethnic ministates after their revolution is accomplished. For example, in

15

Louisiana politician David Duke, one-time candidate for the U.S. Congress, has a long history of white-supremacist, extreme right-wing activities.

1984, the National Association for the Advancement of White People (NAAWP), a militia-connected hate group, published a map called the "National Premise," conceived by David Duke, a former Ku Klux Klan leader and one-time candidate for president. According to the map, Native Americans should be relocated to Oklahoma, Asian Americans to Hawaii, African Americans to parts of Florida and the eastern Gulf Coast, Mexican Americans to the California-Mexico border, Jews to Long Island and Manhattan, Cuban Americans to the Miami area, those of French Canadian heritage to a part of northern New England, and leftover minorities to other parts of the New York metropolitan area.[3]

In general, members of militias and other far-right groups tend to be unsympathetic to the problems of new immigrants in America. For example, in 1981, a paramilitary group in Texas began harassing Vietnamese immigrant fishermen in Galveston Bay, because the paramilitary group thought they were taking business away from white Americans.[4]

Today, white supremacists in the United States are organized into several fringe groups, many of which have at least a minimal cooperative relationship with each other and with local militias. One of the most violent of these racist groups was called the Order, or the Silent Brotherhood. In the 1980s, an informer for the Federal Bureau of Investigation (FBI) revealed that the Order had been producing counterfeit bills; robbing armored cars in Washington state and California; and planning to assassinate former secretary of state Henry Kissinger, a member of the Rothschilds (a Jewish European banking family), and other well-known American Jews. Criminal cases brought against the Order, which was responsible for two murders, eliminated it as a cohesive organization, but Order sympathizers are still active in churches, prisons, and local politics.

There is some evidence that the Order is actually a splinter group of a larger organization known as the Aryan Nations, whose religious arm is the Church of Jesus Christ, Christian, which observes a strict policy of whites only. Its "catechism" is virulently anti-Semitic. At the Aryan Nations' headquarters in Hayden Lake, Idaho, guards wear uniforms similar to those worn by Hitler's secret police, the SS. Sermons often include attacks on American Jews, who are accused of controlling everything from the courts to the banks to the media.

Who Belongs to the Militias?

Surprisingly, many militia members share a host of characteristics with average Americans. According to a 1995 article in the *Philadelphia Daily News*,[5] "The militia movement draws much of its strength from economically struggling white men, many of them veterans, prone to believe in conspiracies, often living in rural areas, fervently defending the right to bear arms." Most members come either from the middle or working classes or are owners of small businesses. "We're talking about people like you and me who feel that they've been pushed too far," says Clark McCauley, a terrorism expert and psychology professor at Bryn Mawr College.[6] Such people may have had been leading unremarkable lives. However, for some time they had been living with a vague feeling of frustration, a sullen anger, and a nagging sense of inferiority. They may first hear about a militia organization at a gun show, then attend a few meetings and discover that there are other people who feel the same frustration and powerlessness. The ideas circulating at the meetings—ideas about a ruthless federal government, a world conspiracy, or corrupt dealings in northeastern cities—offer a chance to focus vague negative feelings on tangible issues. The fact that far-right militias appeal to people who are relatively normal—if resentful and frustrated—makes them all the more disturbing. It shows that they have a potential for a wider membership. People often start out in the more moderate militias, which focus on weekend war games and patriotic family activities. But such activities sometimes bring them into contact with more extreme fringe groups, who work to convert them to their ideas.

Dramatic changes in the nation's economy have also helped convert some people to a more extremist militia mentality. When the mining and timber industries declined in

Extremist literature, including these books on New World Order conspiracy theories and white separatism, are standard fare at many militia events. This 1995 rally was staged in Kalamazoo by the Michigan Militia.

Arizona and Montana, militia groups began to appear. The same was true of certain areas of Michigan and New Hampshire after factories there relocated to Mexico. As people lost jobs, they looked for easy answers and scapegoats. As a result, some were attracted to the conspiracy theories and racist analyses of the far-right militia.

Lately, the right-wing fringes of the militia movement seem to be attracting teenagers. According to another 1995 article in the *Philadelphia Daily News*,[7] this is partly the result of recruiting efforts by militia leaders like Ken Vojtech, founder of the Wayne County Division of the Michigan Militia, who claimed that, at the time, 15 percent to 20 percent of the Michigan Militia was less than twenty years old.

Teenagers who join militias tend to defend their decision as a patriotic gesture. For example, sixteen-year-old David Matthews, a member of the Wayne County branch of the Michigan Militia, saw his decision to join a militia as a quest for true knowledge about America. "Before I joined the militia," he said, "I used to be very ignorant. I thought doing what the government told me was patriotic. . . . We need a militia just to protect people from the threat of tyrannical government. . . . If the people aren't armed, the government doesn't have to listen to them. . . . Buy a gun and get everything you need to protect yourself right now." Matthews vehemently denied that his militia was racist or that anyone associated with it had anything to do with the 1995 bombing of the Alfred P. Murrah Federal Building in Oklahoma City, even though militia sympathizers Timothy McVeigh and Terry Nichols were convicted of the bombing. Such notions, he claimed, were lies spread by the media.

Myths, Strategies, and Rationalizations

Most of the far-right militia groups share the belief that the federal government does not represent the interests of "real" American people and that states' rights, county rights, or even individual rights should replace federal regulations as the supreme law of the land. Accordingly, as a protest against federal regulations, some militia members refuse to pay taxes or use a social security number. They claim that the basic concepts of individual liberties, forged by the Founding Fathers and laid out in the first ten articles of the Bill of Rights, have been betrayed by our current government. They may even say that their identity as Christians prevent them from following certain laws in this country. They believe the time is coming in which "true Christians" such as themselves will end up in mortal combat with "the

20

Beast," which is embodied in the United Nations and the federal government.

Aside from withholding taxes, members of militias and other Patriot groups may express their beliefs by driving without legal license plates or driver's licenses or by violating conservation laws in lands protected by the federal government. Some have even destroyed their marriage licenses and birth certificates as a symbolic gesture against government control. A few have no electricity, telephone, or running water because they say these utilities are controlled by a corporate or government "mafia." Some have stockpiled military-style assault rifles, chemicals, or explosives that are illegal for individuals to own. They might organize combat training groups and home-school their children rather than expose them to differing ideas in the public schools. They are preparing, they say, for the coming war against good Christians like themselves.

The survivalist lifestyle appeals to some militia supporters. As survivalists they opt for completely independent living—often in the wilderness—without any connection to anyone but family and a few friends for food, water, light, heat, safety, or company. Combat soldiers who may find themselves lost for days in a forest or on a mountaintop during war are taught survivalist techniques. Militia members often mimic these actual soldiers, purchasing manuals, camouflage clothing, tents, dried foods, bowie knives, and other weapons needed to survive in the wilderness during wartime. They may justify their survivalist lifestyle by explaining that the time will soon come when the entire infrastructure of the country will break down. There will be war and chaos, and only skilled survivalists will make it through the ordeal.

Many militia members spread propaganda on the Internet or over the radio about a coming takeover of the United States by the United Nations, which they consider a tool of the Jewish world conspiracy, or about concentration camps being built in this country to jail non-Jewish whites who resist. They tell stories about squadrons of mysterious black helicopters patrolling the skies in preparation for a government takeover. They claim to have seen secret symbols on the backs of road signs that will be used by tanks and troops during this supposed takeover, and they say there are troops waiting at the Canadian border to subjugate anyone who resists.

Their interpretations of current events often run wildly counter to those of the mainstream media. After the bombing of the Alfred P. Murrah Federal Building in Oklahoma City, numerous militia leaders made statements on the Internet or the radio claiming that the actual culprits were officials in the federal government hoping to gain more power by increasing fear of terrorists and blaming the incident on militia members. One of the people that made such statements was William Cooper, a far-right radio commentator, who reaches thousands of listeners by broadcasting on Nashville's WWCR through a linkup via shortwave in Arizona.[8]

The idea that the federal government, rather than people connected with the militia movement, was responsible for the Oklahoma bombing seems incredible—not only in light of the fact that paramilitary enthusiast Timothy McVeigh, who attended a meeting of the Michigan Militia, was convicted of the bombing based on ample evidence, but also from the fact that McVeigh had often handed out copies of a favorite novel called *The Turner Diaries*. This extremely racist and violent novel is widely circulated among militia sympathizers. It begins with a similar bombing of a federal building on April 19, the very same day of the year that the Oklahoma bombing actually occurred. April 19 was also the key date in the 1993 disaster in Waco, Texas, which some mark as the impetus for the growth of today's militia movement. The Waco, Texas, event will be described in detail in another chapter.

In what they claim is an attempt to protect individual rights and democracy, members of militias and other right-wing fringe groups have refused to respond to court summonses or obey local sheriffs. Some have threatened journalists, engaged in shootouts with federal agents, murdered liberal spokespersons, bombed abortion clinics and federal buildings, and barricaded themselves into fortresses to avoid arrest. For example, in 1984, Allen Berg, a Jewish radio talk show host who spoke out regularly against right-wing political groups, was shot to death in Denver by members of the Order. And for almost twenty years, various individuals connected with hate groups and the militia movement have made threats on the life of Morris Dees,[9] the chief trial counsel for the Southern Poverty Law Center and its Militia Task Force.

Militia "Law" and Militia "Religion"

Militia groups use a variety of theories, documents, and beliefs to back up their antigovernment or racist opinions. They refer repeatedly to the Bill of Rights and the Articles of Confederation in their arguments. The Articles of Confederation, which predate the Constitution, served as the law of the land from 1781 until 1789, when they were replaced by the Constitution. The Articles of Confederation gave very little power to Congress. Congress could not make laws without the approval of nine of the thirteen states. It could not levy taxes. And even after it passed laws, it could not force the states to follow them. Because the Articles of Confederation stressed states' rights over the authority of the federal government, many militia members prefer them to the Constitution. As far as they are concerned, the Articles are still the supreme law of the United States.

Many militia members claim that the Bible is the first and foremost law of the land. They use passages in it to justify violent acts against abortion clinics, to assert that non-Christians should not have equal rights, or as "proof" that blacks are inferior. Other militia members believe that only the first ten amendments to the Constitution—known as the Bill of Rights—are valid amendments. They are especially obsessed with the Second Amendment, which speaks of the importance of a "well-regulated militia" to maintain the security of each state and of the right of every individual to "bear arms." In fact, ending all gun-control laws are a basic goal of most militia groups, who feel that their freedom is at risk and may have to be defended at any moment with weapons.

Whereas militia groups often quote from the first ten amendments to the Constitution, they tend to question the validity of the next sixteen amendments, which, among other things, guaranteed the citizenship of every person born or naturalized within the United States, abolished slavery, allowed women to vote, and ensured civil rights. This is because many militia members associate full citizenship rights and civil rights with rights for blacks and other minorities, which they see as a threat to "true," meaning white, Americans. They associate the idea of women voting with feminism, and they see feminism as a threat to their definition of the American family, whose unquestioned leader, they feel, should be the father.

The *Protocols of the Elders of Zion*, which supposedly documents the Jewish conspiracy to install a world government, was long ago proved to be a forgery. To many extreme right-wing groups, however, it still serves as evidence of the New World Order conspiracy.

Their interpretations of American history and the foundations of American government tend to be extremely narrow and self-serving. For example, as a reason for not paying taxes, they often cite the Boston Tea Party, which was a rebellion of American colonists against taxes levied on the colonies by England. Antitax militia members claim that their refusal to pay taxes or their paying of taxes with counterfeit currency of their own making come from similar impulses.

Because some militia members believe that America is a Christian nation, they are less likely to support the constitutional principle of the separation of church and state than other Americans. They may go so far as to say that any law that is not based on "God's law" should not be followed.

And they support their ideas with certain documents or legends long ago proven to be false. Chief among these is the *Protocols of the Elders of Zion*,[10] a collection of documents first produced by the secret police in Russia in 1905 and used by the czar and other government officials as "evidence" that Jews were at the heart of a conspiracy to enslave the world. The documents are presented as the actual writings of the elders of Jewish law. In reality, they were adapted from a nineteenth-century anti-Semitic novel.

In the 1920s, these document were revived in the United States by automaker Henry Ford, who had an obsessive hatred of Jews and was willing to believe that the *Protocols* were legitimate documents. Ford sold more than half a million copies of the *Protocols* in the 1920s. However, during World War II, the need for Americans to work together to defeat Nazi-controlled Europe made the anti-Semitic ideas of Ford and others unpopular. The *Protocols* sank back into obscurity. Then in recent years, extreme-right groups, many of whom are associated with the militia movement (as well as some blacks associated with the Nation of Islam, which propounds various anti-Semitic theories), republished and distributed these documents. They are popular reading material among some militia supporters and members of other Patriot groups. They are also quoted by adherents of certain religious groups strongly associated with the militia movement, such as Christian Identity, a theology with roots stretching back to England in the nineteenth century.

The founders of the set of ideas that led to the modern Christian Identity movement believed that white Christians, not Jews, are the true descendants of the ancient Hebrews. In the United States, these beliefs evolved into a philosophical position that Jews are Satan's biological descendants and that other minorities are subhuman soulless species created

26

before Adam and Eve.[11] Christian Identity asserts that Jesus Christ and other "true" Hebrews were Aryans, a theoretical race of "pure" white people that originally inhabited what is now Scandinavia and northern Europe and for which there is no scientific or historical evidence. The leading Christian Identity movement today is the Aryan Nations, which in turn produced most members of the extremely violent subgroup the Order.

The Roots of Today's Militia Movement

Three enduring mentalities in American culture have led to today's militia movement. They are racism, hyperpatriotism, and religious fanaticism. In *The Party of Fear*, his history of the right wing in America, David H. Bennett traces racism in this country from a secret society known as the Order of the Star-Spangled Banner, which later was called the Know-Nothings, because its members were pledged to secrecy.

The Know-Nothings were active as early as the mid-nineteenth century. Their goal was to "purify" the nation, which they felt was being corrupted by "un-American" non-Protestant immigrants. The Know-Nothings were part of a current in American culture that scholars call nativism. This means that they had a narrow idea of which residents of the country constituted "real" Americans and that they hoped to limit rights, property, and citizenship to these people. According to Bennett, "The picture of the United States as a unique and gifted land, a garden of Eden that must be preserved against the encroachment of sinners, informed the work of [the Know-Nothings], the most important nativist movement of the nineteenth century."[12] Like the far-right militia, the Know-Nothings had an idealized version of America that they thought they could realize by illegal, militant activism.

The racist and nativist ideas of many of today's militias can be traced back to the Know-Nothings, a group that formed in the mid-nineteenth century in response to the huge influx of Irish Catholics.

The main targets of the Know-Nothings were Irish Americans, because at that time the Catholic Irish were one of the largest minorities in the country. By the beginning of the twentieth century, the focus of racist activism had changed. Racist paranoia was then directed at the millions of immigrants pouring into the country from southern and eastern Europe—especially Italians and Jews. One group, known as the Ku Klux Klan, came to the fore of these nativist-racist organizations.

Originally organized after the Civil War, the Klan disbanded in 1869 and was reincarnated in 1915. The new organization had much in common with today's far-right groups. Like many of them, it favored racial pride, patriotic propaganda, and secret rituals. It was open only to native-born, white Protestant males. This new incarnation lacked central leadership, but it did expand haphazardly. The new Klan targeted blacks, Jews, Roman Catholics, liberals, and

The Ku Klux Klan, shown here in a 1923 parade in Tulsa, Oklahoma, formed after the Civil War to oppose the emancipation of enslaved blacks. Since that time, the Klan has gone through several incarnations but has continued to express its racist view of the United States as a white Christian nation.

union members. After peaking around 1925, the Klan once again faded from history. But during the civil rights movement of the 1960s, local organizations using the name Ku Klux Klan formed throughout the South to oppose freedom activists and protest civil rights reform efforts. Repeatedly, these organizations had violent encounters with blacks, civil rights workers, and the government. Some Klan members later moved into the militia movement, with some becoming leaders in the 1990s.

The 1920s also saw one of the most paranoid patriotic crusades of the century. In January 1920, thousands of workers, journalists, and political activists were arrested and accused of being communist sympathizers. Often the arrests were based on little evidence. These days became known as

Alger Hiss takes the oath before the House Un-American Activities Committee hearings. The hearings ruined the careers and lives of numerous individuals who were "suspected" of holding Communist sympathies. Hiss was accused of selling U.S. military secrets to the Soviet government.

the Red Scare, a symptom of growing anxiety about communism on the part of some Americans. The Red Scare overlapped with a movement in the country that was suspicious and distrustful of new immigrants and unskilled workers, accusing many of them of being "bolsheviks," anarchists, and political terrorists. Thirty years later, in the 1950s, communist witch-hunts led by Senator Joseph McCarthy helped spread an atmosphere of distrust and paranoia throughout the nation once more. Today, fear and hatred of left-wing ideologies is a constant refrain of far-right militias. Sometimes, when militia members have been accused of violent acts, they have defended themselves by asserting that they were only acting patriotically to defend America from "socialism."

As has already been explained, religious fanaticism is central to much of the far-right militia mentality. Movements like Christian Identity assert that the Bible is subject to no interpretation but their own. These interpretations are then used to justify paramilitary activities and sometimes violence.

Most far-right Christian militia members are fundamentalists, who believe in a literal interpretation of the Bible. In this country, fundamentalism's roots lie in the Evangelical Protestant movements of Great Britain and North America that began several hundred years ago. These movements called for strict morals, more plainspoken religious practices, and the supreme authority of the Bible. In 1909, twelve books called *The Fundamentals* written by fervent Evangelists with very conservative religious views were distributed in the United States and abroad. Bible institutes, such as the Los Angeles Bible Institute and the Moody Bible Institute in Chicago, began teaching the doctrines expressed in the twelve books.

Fundamentalism grew considerably throughout the century. Recently, some of the movement's more conservative elements became politically motivated and formed what is generally referred to as the Christian Right. The Christian Right is a loose coalition of conservative Protestants that has developed into a huge voting bloc within the last twenty-five years. The coalition now has some strong allies in the Republican Party. The goals of most of its members include bringing prayer back into the schools, outlawing abortion and homosexual rights, and promoting traditional family values.

The vast majority of the people who belong to the Christian Right are not involved in militias or any paramilitary movement, but religious fundamentalists have helped the Patriot movement grow. Organizations like Pat Robertson's Christian Coalition, which has several hundred thousand members, help feed the paranoia, conspiracy theories, and sense of divine mission that keep some far-right militias going. Robertson, a television evangelist, wrote a 1991 book called *The New World Order*, which was a best-seller to the tune of half a million copies. This book contributed a great deal to militia paranoia. In its pages Robertson posits an international conspiracy of bankers, members of the Federal Reserve System, the Trilateral Commission, and the United Nations, which is poised to take over the world.

The Militia Movement as a Whole

When it comes down to it, it's hard to create a simple definition of today's extreme right-wing movements. As David H. Bennett has pointed out in his book on the history of the far right in America, the culture of the militia movement comes from disparate sources that have existed for a long time in the United States. The movement is "a shifting mixture of survivalist loners and self-styled constitutional experts preaching against federal tyranny, of neo-Nazi theorists and Christian Identity ministers, of young white-supremacist toughs and their adult mentors, of fragmentary Klan chapters and fierce tax resisters, of angry travelers on the gun-show circuit and manipulators of the far-Right radio, video and Internet world."[13]

Although some members of extreme right-wing groups identify themselves first and foremost as Christians, others are focused mainly on race. They may be members of the

Skinhead groups, such as this one in former East Germany, are at the most extreme and violent end of the Patriot movement spectrum.

Aryan Nations. Some are neo-Nazis who shave their heads and listen to violent, white-power music. Others are associated with one of the many different local Ku Klux Klan groups.

Most militia members are less concerned with race and more obsessed with the power of the federal government. Their political affiliations range in degree of extremism. Some are members of the John Birch Society, an ultraconservative but nonviolent society that was founded in 1958 to combat socialist and communist ideas. A large number belong either to the National Rifle Association or to other gun-lobbying organizations. Virtually all feel that the gun-control laws in this country are unjust. Almost all militia members mix religion and politics. They hold beliefs that range from the racist-nativist ideas of Christian Identity and Aryan Nations to the relatively mild conspiracy theories of Pat Robertson.

Militia groups with racist ideologies or extremist religious views usually keep these controversial ideas in the background. They've found that they have more success in recruiting by concentrating on their appeal to middle- and working-class people who feel economically and politically cheated.[14] They focus their activities on protecting the right to bear arms and opposing taxes, government regulations, abortion, homosexual rights, and the current system of public education. Or they stress seemingly benign evangelical activities and community social gatherings with a strong emphasis on family values.

The far-right militia movement is difficult to define as a whole. But the groups usually share the following characteristics:

1. They are motivated by an intense hatred of the federal government.
2. They are interested in the use of private, sometimes illegal paramilitary activities to accomplish goals.
3. They claim to be ultrapatriotic.
4. They rely on extremist religious beliefs, conspiracy theories, or far-fetched interpretations of the ideas at the basis of our nation's government to rationalize their actions.

Jesse James claimed that the outcome of the Civil War and the crisis it caused in the lives of Southern rural people forced them into an adversarial relationship with government, the courts, the banks, and big business. Militia members, who often feel victimized, exploited, or ignored by contemporary America, have a similar rationalizing mentality. What they are doing, they say, is what anyone would do if they were caught between a rock and a hard place. They believe that their well-being and their values are being subverted by a monstrous government supported by a lying media and greedy big business. They believe that their race and religion are under siege. In their minds, illicit small-scale underground activities and individual acts of violence are often seen as their only choice.

CHAPTER 2

THE CATALYSTS: RUBY RIDGE AND WACO

Paranoid fears can be self-fulfilling. Sometimes the very actions one takes to prevent them from coming true can make them a reality. In a sense, that's what happened to Randy Weaver and David Koresh. Both feared the federal government so obsessively that they took extreme measures to protect themselves from it. Step by horrible step, these measures put them at its mercy. The psychology shared by Randy Weaver and David Koresh and the situations into which it led them are symptomatic of the militia mentality. In fact, what happened to these men became catalysts for today's militia movement, galvanizing and organizing people angered by their stories.

Randy Weaver and Ruby Ridge

Weaver was a veteran and a survivalist, a firm believer in the idea that the United States was being controlled by ZOG, the so-called Zionist Occupation Government. Although he had been raised a Baptist, his fears about the government and an intense desire for a guiding light and a central purpose in life led him toward extreme beliefs. Eventually, Weaver and his wife became members of Christian Identity. Through their church fellowship they claimed to have discovered that America was the new Jerusalem and that the only true government this land could have must be strictly Bible-based. Like other Christian Identity followers, the Weavers had a narrow, very specific interpretation of the Scriptures. They believed that the Bible was written solely for white people who would be the principal benefactors of the Second Coming, when Christ returned to Earth. They also believed that, as predicted by the Book of Revelation, the end of the world as we now know it, ushered in by the Battle of Armageddon, was coming. Wars, diseases, famines, and natural disasters would devastate America. ZOG would wage a ruthless war against all good Christians. After this bloody apocalypse, true believers like the Weavers and other "soldier-saints" of Christian Identity would be united with God—whether they lived or died. They refer to God using the Hebrew word *Yahweh*, which means "He Who Is," which the ancient Hebrews used because they thought the real name for God was too sacred to speak aloud. The members of Christian Identity believe that they are the real descendants of the ancient Hebrews and have thus adopted the name.

Randy Weaver often considered the fact that his faith might lead the corrupt government of ZOG to murder him or his family. He claimed that this did not matter to him, because he felt he and his family would die in union with Yahweh. One major step in his development as a radical Christian Identity believer was to move his family from his home state of Iowa to the mountains of northern Idaho. There the land was remote and untouched, although a large percentage of it was federal preserve and thus belonged to the federal government. Idaho allowed home schooling, so Weaver's children would not have to be subjected to ideas he considered immoral. Weaver built his family home near Hayden Lake, not far from the headquarters of Aryan Nations, where he attended some meetings.

The Weavers lived on an isolated mountaintop called Ruby Ridge in sparsely populated Boundary County, which has barely eight thousand inhabitants. Only twenty-nine of

Federal agents and members of the media tour the scene at Randy Weaver's remote hideout at Ruby Ridge. In the foreground are weapons confiscated from the Weavers.

them were nonwhite.[1] Randy Weaver's neighbors had varying opinions of him. Some respected his independence; others saw him as an abrasive extremist. In 1988, he ran for sheriff. Although he lost, he did receive 102 of the 400 votes cast.

In preparation for what they believed was the coming apocalypse, the Weavers bought guns and ammunition, including two Ruger Mini-14 semiautomatics.[2] Weaver also built a rude cabin of plywood in the mountains. Its electricity was supplied by a generator, and water came from a nearby spring and from melted snow.

In 1989, Weaver's gnawing fears about the federal government suddenly seemed to come true. It started when he met a fellow Christian Identity follower named Gus Magisono at an Aryan Nations get-together. Magisono told Weaver he needed to buy some sawed-off shotguns to advance the aims of Christian Identity. Weaver agreed to sell him the guns and, as requested, sawed down the barrels. When the transaction with Magisono was completed, Weaver was arrested. He had been set up. Magisono was actually a federal government informant named Kenneth Fadeley who was hoping to infiltrate the white supremacist movement and foil terrorist plans.

After Weaver was arrested, the FBI offered him a deal. They would drop the gun-running charges against him if he agreed to provide them with information on the white supremacist movement. Weaver refused and was indicted, but he never appeared for trial. Instead, he took his entire family to his remote cabin in the mountains. From the beginning, law enforcement officials realized they would have a hard time getting him out of there. On one side was a cliff that dropped several hundred feet. The other side could only be reached by an abandoned logging road.

Armed confrontations with survivalists had resulted in tragedy in the past. The 1983 shootout with Gordon Kahl in North Dakota was one example. After that incident, the rules for managing encounters with white supremacists and survivalists had been revised by the U.S. Marshals Service. In situations that were likely to lead to dangerous shootouts, the marshals were to try to avoid armed confrontation and to use negotiation, watchful waiting, and containment.[3] William F. Degan, the U.S. marshal involved in the Weaver case, vowed to arrest Weaver for skipping his court date, but he also planned to take his time about it. He hoped to convince Weaver to surrender by sending messages to him by mail, through friends, or through his lawyer. A year passed and Weaver's wife had her fourth child without the family leaving the vicinity of the cabin. Still Degan hesitated, because he feared that a violent confrontation could endanger not only the lives of his deputies but also those of Weaver's wife and children. After all, Weaver's three older children—all minors—were armed, just like their father.

Meanwhile, the Weavers survived on food and other supplies brought to them by as many as fifty local supporters. Through the mail and their lawyer, Weaver sent bold messages of defiance. "Whether we live or whether we die," Weaver wrote the marshals, "we will not obey your lawless government."[4] Slowly but surely, Weaver was becoming a hero to those who thought the way he did. Meanwhile, the mainstream press was beginning to chide Marshal Degan for procrastinating. When was he going to arrest Weaver for defying the laws of the country?

Seventeen months into the siege, in August 1992, Degan and some other marshals decided to climb the ridge for a closer look at what was going on. The men were dressed in camouflage. When the Weaver's dog Striker started barking,

Weaver's fourteen-year-old son, Sam and a friend of the family named Kevin Harris left the cabin to investigate. No one has ever proved who fired the first shot, but apparently one of the marshals shot the dog in an attempt to keep him from revealing their whereabouts. A gun battle followed. When it was over, Sam Weaver and Marshal Degan were dead.

After this incident, Weaver must have felt that the forces of ZOG had already been unleashed upon him in all their fury. Nevertheless, the next day would bring more tragedy. Because of Degan's death, the FBI flew its elite Hostage Rescue Team to the scene.[5] These agents had new orders to shoot on sight any male leaving the cabin. When FBI agent Lon Horiuchi spotted Weaver and Harris as they returned from viewing Sam's corpse in a nearby shed, he fired. The shot blew off half the face of Weaver's wife, Vicki, who was standing at the cabin door with her baby in her arms.

On August 26, five days after the death of Sam Weaver, negotiations between Weaver and the FBI were still at a standstill.[6] Weaver would not respond at all. Swarms of FBI agents, National Guardsmen, U.S. marshals, police, and deputies had converged on the area. A roadblock cut off all nonofficial access to the ridge. Protesters holding placards that accused the "feds" of being tyrants assembled at the scene. What is more, a significant proportion of the townspeople were on Weaver's side and weren't afraid to talk about it to their neighbors or the press.

Members of the Aryan Nations stationed themselves at the roadblock. They shouted slurs at FBI agents and handed out copies of a letter that Vicki Weaver had written to the Aryan Nations in 1990 asking for their help when her husband was pressured to work with federal agents. The members of the Aryan Nations were joined by a small group of violent skinheads and other extreme rightists who felt a passionate identification with Weaver. Their statements were plastered all over the media. What had begun as an isolated incident was reaching a larger and larger audience.

On August 26, James "Bo" Gritz, who had been a Special Forces commander during the Vietnam War, offered to go up to the cabin to speak to Weaver.[7] Gritz said he had known Weaver while in combat. They shared many values and beliefs. Perhaps he could do something to bring the siege to an end.

Gritz's entrance into the Ruby Ridge saga helped elevate the incident to the level of militia legend and make Gritz a well-known figure in the far-right Patriot movement. He had been a Green Beret commander in Vietnam, and because he had led some forays into Southeast Asia in search of prisoners of war, many people said he was the inspiration for the character Rambo. In 1988, he had been the vice presidential candidate of the extreme-right Populist Party, which had chosen former Klansman David Duke as their presidential candidate. He had also been a close ally of Pete Peters, a leader of Christian Identity. Although Gritz later rejected Duke and tried to distance himself from Christian Identity and Patriot organizations that were blatantly racist, many of his public statements echoed the far-right Christian-Patriot agenda. Gritz referred to President George Bush as King George and accused him of being part of a satanic conspiracy that wanted to turn a Christian nation into a corporate entity. At the Ruby Ridge siege, he shamelessly promoted his own political ambitions by having "Bo Gritz for President" signs put up. He even handed out his own "arrest warrants" charging the Idaho governor, the FBI director, and other officials with the murder of both Degan and Sam Weaver.

Three days after Gritz's arrival, the FBI decided to let him talk to Weaver and even act as one of the principal negotiators. When Gritz came back down from the ridge after a long conversation with Weaver, he told the FBI that Weaver's wife was dead and Weaver and Harris had been wounded.

Over the next few days, Gritz learned Weaver's account of the death of Sam Weaver and Degan. Weaver said that Sam had shot Degan after the dog had been shot by the federal agents. There had been nothing to identify them as agents. They were wearing camouflage when they sneaked onto his property. After Degan was shot, Weaver, Sam, and Harris ran for the cabin. It was then that Sam was shot in the arm and the back.

Later, Weaver's daughter Sara sent a letter describing a somewhat different version. It said that Harris admitted to shooting Degan after Sam had been shot. The next day, Vicki had been shot as Weaver and Harris were returning from the cabin after going to the shed to view Sam's body. Vicki had been holding the cabin door open for them.

On August 30, a badly wounded Harris surrendered.[8] A day later, Weaver surrendered as well. His two older daughters and his baby were not in bad condition, but he was suffering from a bullet wound in the armpit. He was treated for the wound and then imprisoned.

At the trial that followed, Harris, who had been charged with murder, conspiracy, and firearms violations, was acquitted. Weaver was convicted only for failing to appear in court. After a total of eighteen months in jail, he was free. The government's failure to convict Weaver of serious charges was seen by the far right as an important victory. The trial also became symbolic of the dangerous tensions between far-right individuals and the federal government, casting the FBI in a bad light.

Randy Weaver testifies during his 1995 trial as to the events that led to the lengthy siege and subsequent deaths of his son and wife and a local marshal.

During the trial the judge censured the FBI for obstructing justice and ignoring the basic rights of the defendants. The FBI had, it seemed, removed objects from the scene of the crime before photographing it; it had taken its time in turning over other information; and it had destroyed at least one document relating to Ruby Ridge. Even the summons to appear in court that Weaver had disobeyed, which had led to the standoff, was proved to have errors in it. It contained the wrong date. Eventually, Weaver sued the federal government. Because of the mistakes in its handling of the situation, the federal government settled, paying Weaver $100,000 and each of his three daughters $1 million.

In 1997, an official named E. Michael Kahoe[9] was sentenced to eighteen months in prison for shredding an FBI report critical of the department's actions during the Ruby Ridge encounter. This had been done to prevent Weaver's

44

lawyers from reading the report, which, among other things, criticized guidelines allowing agents on the scene to fire at adults, whether or not they were a threat to the agents. The report said that the FBI guidelines for the siege were, in fact, unconstitutional.

Such a dishonest and sloppy approach on the part of a government agency made sensational fodder for the media. By the time the trial was over, several prestigious newspapers, including the *New York Times*, had had harsh words for the way Ruby Ridge had been handled. Clumsy strategies on the parts of law enforcers, the FBI's dishonesty, Weaver's appeal as a simple family man, and the disapproval of the mainstream press undoubtedly brought thousands of people into the Patriot camp. In fact, most experts see Ruby Ridge as the first real catalyst in the birth of today's militia movement. An editorial in the *Miami Herald*[10] stated, "The case of Mr. Weaver, a self-styled 'white separatist' . . . has become a cause célèbre for the right-wing militia movement. Indeed, for the political right in the West, 'Remember Ruby Ridge' has become a rallying cry for the 1990s, much as 'Remember Kent State' galvanized the peace movement of the 1970s." The Kent State reference was to a much-discussed event of 1970 in which National Guard troops killed four students at a demonstration against the Vietnam War at Kent State University in Ohio.

Meanwhile, other forces were working hand in hand with Ruby Ridge to win new converts to the militia movement. Even while Gritz acted as a negotiator at Ruby Ridge, his supporters were holding rallies in several major regional cities to elect him president. Later, Gritz's supporters sold videotapes and transcripts of his press conference at Ruby Ridge to boost his image as a leader in the far rights' fight for what they consider their constitutional rights. Gritz was

Randy Weaver (center) and Bo Gritz (to the immediate right of Weaver) crash an antiextremist conference in Montana in 1996.

determined to make his stand against the New World Order a national issue. In speeches around the country, he called for the end of income tax, the destruction of the Federal Reserve System, and a new Christian America. Gritz also began offering people interested in the militia movement a chance to participate (for a $100 fee) in a military-style training program called SPIKE (Specially Trained Individuals for Key Events). According to Gritz, the course was designed to empower those who do not feel secure about safeguarding their constitutional rights. At a 1995 rally in the San Joaquin Valley, Gritz and a local National Guard sergeant who'd been charged and acquitted of possession of illegal assault weapons inspired the crowd by burning a United Nations flag.

Militia of Montana cofounder John Trochmann speaks with an attendee at the Self-Sufficiency and Preparedness Expo in Spokane, Washington, in February 1997. Trochmann's involvement with Weaver during the Ruby Ridge incident and trial was a major impetus for his decision to found a private militia.

Another leader connected both with the Ruby Ridge incident and the militia movement was John Trochmann. Trochmann and his wife, Carolyn, had been close friends of the Weavers. During the siege, they helped provide the family with supplies. When the case ended, Trochmann began working in earnest with family members, using a large mailing list to build a paramilitary movement called the Militia of Montana, which, at the beginning of 1994, became an official organization. The Militia of Montana became one of the earliest and most powerful of the new Patriot paramilitary groups. Eventually, it would offer videotapes, manuals, and other media detailing guerrilla warfare techniques, including attacking corporations and kidnapping public officials, and suggesting other strategies to bring down the present system of governing the nation. Some of its members later threatened state judges and prosecutors and had armed confrontations with law enforcers. The Militia of Montana and other groups like it might never have gotten off the ground if the Ruby Ridge incident hadn't occurred. At the time, law enforcement officials were unaware of how powerfully their botched confrontation would reverberate. When they did realize what was happening, it was too late.

Waco

The FBI's clumsiness in handling the Ruby Ridge affair gave the far-right militia movement that much more justification for its beliefs and actions. So much about the incident was vague. Who had behaved more treacherously: Randy Weaver, when he sold illegally sawed-off shotguns, or the FBI, when they asked him to saw them off? Who had shot first during the siege: the Weavers or government agents? There was opportunity for finger-pointing on both sides. Unfortunately, another important and controversial incident occurred only fifteen

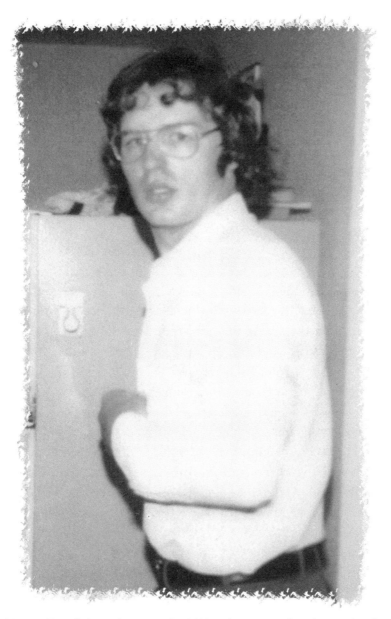

Vernon Howell, better known as David Koresh, was not directly associated with militias, but his extreme religious views and willingness to use violence to oppose the U.S. government has made him a hero to some extreme-right groups.

months later. Militia supporters still refer to it as the "Waco massacre."

Vernon Howell was born in Houston, Texas, in 1959 to a mother of fifteen. Howell never met his father. His grandparents raised him. People who knew him as a teenager said that he was deeply religious but also interested in rock music—so much so that he became a skilled musician. Howell excelled at sports, playing end on the school football team. Even so, his childhood was not a happy one. He was dyslexic, and his grades were poor. After the ninth grade, he dropped out of school.

As an adult, Howell's religious preoccupations led him into the Seventh-Day Adventist Church, to which his mother had belonged. This fundamentalist church had been founded in the nineteenth century. Its doctrine focuses on fervent faith in the Second Coming of Christ on Earth and the observance of the Sabbath on Saturday, rather than on Sunday. After a while, Howell found the church too moderate. He spent a couple of years in Hollywood trying unsuccessfully to make it as a rock musician, then returned to Texas and joined the Branch Davidians, a radical religious sect that had broken away from the Seventh-Day Adventists. Branch Davidian theology stressed interpretation of the seven seals mentioned in the Book of Revelation, which is the last book of the New Testament. The purpose of Revelation is to prepare Christians for God's return to Earth before which it is believed there will be great destruction.

In several chapters of Revelation, a book with seven seals is described. When a lamb begins opening these seals, the wrath of God is unleashed upon the Earth and even the stars fall from the sky. All of this is in preparation for the Second Coming, which will lead to the Day of Judgment, an event that will occur in full when the final, seventh seal is broken.

The ATF attack on the Branch Davidian compound
seemed to the group to justify its belief in the arrival
of the Apocalypse foretold in the Book of Revelation.

After Howell got involved with the Branch Davidians, members came to believe that they had to prepare for the opening of the seven seals with a survivalist lifestyle. According to the FBI, that is the reason they began stockpiling sophisticated assault weapons, some of which are illegal for individuals to own. In the minds of the Branch Davidians, the ultimate confrontation between Good and Evil was coming. They wanted to be as ready for it as possible.

Although the Branch Davidians preparing for violence from outsiders they considered nonbelievers, disagreements within their own ranks sometimes led to dangerous confrontations. Howell had been having an affair with Lois Roden, the prophetess of the sect. In the mid-1980s, when Lois Roden died, Howell got involved in a struggle with her son, George Roden, for control of the sect. In 1987, at the Branch Davidian compound near Waco, Texas, their disagreements led to a gun battle. Howell and seven others were charged with attempted murder. In the end, Howell's charges were dismissed, and the other seven people were acquitted. By 1990, it became clear that Howell had won the struggle. He was now the head prophet of the Branch Davidian sect.

In 1991, Howell changed his name to David Koresh, a reference to biblical characters. David was the king of the Jews and Israel and is thought to be the father of the Hebrew people. Koresh, or Cyrus, was the King of Persia. It was he who allowed the Jews to return from their exile in Babylon to Israel to rebuild the Temple of Solomon. Koresh stated on court documents that he had changed his name for publicity and business purposes, but he later made it clear that he considered himself the head of the biblical House of David. Koresh also began believing that his appointed task was to teach people about the seven seals and other truths in the

Book of Revelation. He was filled with anguish that the mainstream Christian denominations did not seem to accept him. Eventually, this anguish turned to a kind of mania. Koresh began to believe that he was Jesus Christ.

Koresh's sense of a divine mission galvanized many of the members of his sect, who truly believed he was their prophet. To many he seemed passionate and inspired, an irresistible force that gave their lives focus and courage. An ex-member of the cult described him as "a very charismatic speaker. . . . He had what would seem to be a very, very sharp mind, but oddly sharp—almost schizophrenic."

"[Koresh's] strength over people," the same ex-follower went on to say, "is that he was offering very simple answers. He convinced his followers that the world was going to end and that the key to their salvation was to do what he said—just believe in those things, and you'll be fine."[11]

Things didn't work out that way, however. Koresh's leadership led his disciples into more and more dangerous territory. In 1992, the government began an eight-month investigation of the sect. The Branch Davidians had been purchasing large quantities of weapon parts and ammunition. They'd also been buying ingredients used to make explosives and such survivalist supplies as night-vision sensors. When a UPS parcel was discovered to contain hand grenades, the Bureau of Alcohol, Tobacco and Firearms (ATF) got involved. Agents secured a search warrant and planned a large-scale raid of the Branch Davidian compound for February 28, 1993.

But someone accidentally tipped off the cult to the ATF's planned raid. News of the raid had leaked to the media, and a cameraman assigned by his station to cover the action got lost on a back road. After asking a mailman for directions to the compound, he said something to the effect of, "You better get out of here because there's a National Guard helicopter over at Texas State Technical Institute, and they're going to have a big shootout with the religious nuts."[12] His remark couldn't have been more insensitive or ill-timed. The mailman was Koresh's brother-in-law.[13] He quickly warned Koresh of the raid.

Once again government agents were faced with a bad situation. Apparently, they were aware that Koresh had been warned about the raid before it began. Nevertheless, they decided to go ahead with it, never imagining that Koresh's weaponry and readiness were on a level beyond their own. It was later revealed that the Branch Davidians had an arsenal that included AR-15 semiautomatic rifles, Israeli assault rifles, Russian AK-47s, and .50-caliber weapons.

The raid started to go wrong from the moment armed government commandos began their assault on the compound. Helicopters intended to distract the Davidians while the ATF invaded the compound arrived late. During the shootout that followed, four ATF agents lost their lives. About fifteen others were wounded. Reports as to who had fired first differed. The agents said that the Branch Davidians had begun firing before the commandos could even get out of their trailers. Koresh later claimed that the agents had fired the first shots. Later in the day, gunfire broke out again when three cult members exited the compound; one member was killed, another wounded, and the third taken into custody. In a telephone interview with a newspaper that followed, Koresh said that he and some other members of the sect had also been wounded in the gun battle.

In the fifty-one-day standoff that followed, Koresh and his followers remained locked inside the compound, while government agents used every nonviolent technique they

Top is a view of the Branch Davidian compound as it appeared during the siege. Below, foundations and a few partial walls are all that remain after the fire set by the Davidians as their final act of defiance.

could muster to force them out. These included telephone negotiations, cutting off the compound's electricity, and broadcasting obnoxious noises to disturb the Davidians' sleep. Eventually, some children and other Branch Davidians left the compound. But Koresh, who was wounded, as well as a core of followers, stubbornly resisted. In a telephone interview, Koresh claimed to be Christ come again to Earth to reveal the mysteries of the Book of Revelation. He spoke of the apocalypse to come, and rather than claiming to be above the law, said in effect that he himself was the law.

Sensational newspaper reports about the Branch Davidians had appeared the day before the ATF raid. These reports claimed that Koresh was polygamous, meaning that he had more than one wife. They also claimed that Koresh was sexually abusing minors. Although Koresh admitted to being polygamous, a choice he ascribed to his religious beliefs, he denied the allegations of sexual abuse.

The standoff near Waco attracted fanatics, tourists, and opportunists. Vendors sold T-shirts and bumper stickers with such slogans as "WACO—We Ain't Coming Out." Louis Beam, who had led the Klan group that terrorized Vietnamese fishermen in Texas, came to Waco to cover the event for a Christian Identity periodical called the *Jubilee*.[14] His position was that the Bureau of Alcohol, Tobacco, and Firearms was a villainous, totalitarian organization that was intruding on the rights of the Branch Davidians. At the roadblock that the government agents had set up near the compound, pickets raised signs that proclaimed, "ATF Kills Babies."[15] Other people came merely out of curiosity, excited by the prospect of a Hollywood-style conflict between the government and some rebels.

Meanwhile, FBI agents, who had taken over the siege from the ATF, began planning another raid. This one, they hoped, would not lead to any deaths. The basic strategy was to pierce the walls of the compound with armored tanks and shoot tear gas inside it, forcing the Branch Davidians out.

On April 19, shortly before 6 A.M., the FBI warned the Davidians by telephone that they would be gassed if they didn't surrender immediately. Ten minutes later, the armored tanks began rolling toward the compound. Although the Davidians fired on them, no FBI agent was harmed. As the tanks began to ram the walls of the compound and pump in tear gas, an enormous blaze erupted. Fanned by the wind, it reduced the compound to cinders, killing more than eighty Branch Davidians, including Koresh and seventeen children.[16] Evidence later produced in court indicated that the Davidians set the fire themselves, apparently as part of a mass suicide.

Attorney General Janet Reno, who had approved the raid, said she had been aware that Koresh might order the Davidians to commit suicide rather than surrender. Nevertheless, she felt the raid had been justified. It had been an attempt, she said, to end the siege without undue violence and to save the lives of children inside who were living in unhealthy conditions.

However, the lawyers for Koresh and his chief lieutenant, who also died in the blaze, strongly disagreed. "This ripping open the walls and injecting tear gas where there were a number of women and children was senseless and did not serve to bring about the peaceful resolution that everybody wanted," said Koresh's lawyer Dick DeGuerin.[17] The lawyer also said he was convinced that, in the initial raid, the ATF agents, not the Davidians, had fired the first shots.

Although President Bill Clinton defended the actions of the FBI, he called for a joint probe of the incident by the Justice Department and the Treasury Department, which is in charge of the ATF. Meanwhile, the National Rifle Association and other pro-gun groups began using what had happened at Waco to lobby against gun control and for an armed American citizenry. Postings to the Internet by pro-gun Americans mushroomed. Polls showed that the level of anger against the federal government was very high, and survivalists, paramilitarists, and ultra-patriots weren't going to take what had happened lying down. They promised Reno and the FBI a much bloodier struggle if a similar standoff ever happened again.

Militia sympathizers with media savvy got a lot of mileage out of the Waco incident. Linda Thompson,[18] an Indianapolis attorney, offered to defend Koresh during the siege. When a plan to work with Koresh's lawyer backfired, she had begun sending faxes in the name of her "unorganized Militia of the United States of America" that called for citizen soldiers to assemble near Waco.

After the siege, Thompson dedicated herself to the Waco issue in earnest. She converted her law office into the American Justice Federation, the purpose of which was to distribute pamphlets and videos on Waco, the New World Order, and the federal government. Two videotapes she made about Waco, Waco: *The Big Lie* and *Waco II: The Big Lie Continues*, tried to prove that the Waco incident was an attack on religious freedom and part of a government conspiracy to disarm ordinary Americans. The tapes also asserted that ATF agents had tried to murder the Davidians in cold blood. Thompson claimed that her first tape contained footage showing that a tank had thrown flames, not gas, into the compound. However, the interpretation of the footage has been widely disputed, including by many on the extreme right. They say that what looks like flames coming from the tanks was actually something reflective, like a piece of metal, that fell on the tank as it pulled away.[19]

According to Morris Dees, author of the *Gathering Storm: America's Militia Threat*, Waco and Ruby Ridge stoked furious resentment over the Brady Bill when it was passed later that year. The Brady Bill was a gun-control law that required a five-day waiting period and a background check for anyone trying to buy a gun. To show their disapproval of the bill, the National Rifle Association made as much as they could of the Ruby Ridge and Waco tragedies. They played upon the fears that Ruby Ridge and Waco had caused in many American gun-owners, who felt that Washington did not understand their needs or values and could soon become their enemy. More and more of these gun-owners became convinced that they themselves might lose the right to bear arms. This attracted them to the ideas of the far-right militias, which offered the security of banding together in private armies to resist federal powers.

Shortly after Waco, far-right militias in several states really took off. Their clashes with the government, the media, and private individuals became more frequent and more serious. The movement was building toward a devastating climax, the bombing of the Alfred P. Murrah Federal Building in Oklahoma City. However, disgruntled gun-owners were far from alone in leading the militia movement toward this tragedy. Some key spokespeople and activists of the movement helped. Their strategies recruited thousands to their cause and created and shaped the recent journey of the militia movement toward large-scale terrorism.

CHAPTER 3

THE MILITIA MOVEMENT'S LEADING FIGURES

The activists of the far-right militia movement come from many different places in the country and many different walks of life. The movement has no formal unity or central authority. However, certain charismatic figures have been able to attract support for the values of the far-right militias. Some of them have been working to spread their ideas and accomplish their goals for more than a generation. A small percentage have been directly tied to violent acts.

Fathers of the Movement

From his highly guarded office in Hayden Lake, Idaho, eighty-plus Richard Butler rules the Aryan Nations with an iron hand. Butler founded Aryan Nations in 1973, two years after taking control of the Church of Jesus Christ, Christian, a leading Christian Identity church in California. Butler moved the headquarters of the church from Southern California to Hayden Lake because the mix of races in California was counter to his ideal of an all-white America. His dream was to make Hayden Lake the capital of a five-state Aryan nation composed of Oregon, Wyoming, Montana, Idaho, and Washington.

Although Butler's dream never came true, he did create a national network of far-right sympathizers by maintaining strong ties with local incarnations of the Ku Klux Klan and some former members of the American Nazi Party. His

Aryan Nations founder Richard Butler in a 1985 photo taken under the symbol of his Church of Jesus Christ, Christian.

organization, Aryan Nations, preaches white Christian superiority and Jewish villainy and inferiority. It also predicts a race war in which white Christians will have to defend themselves against the satanic Jews and members of the nonwhite races. For that reason, Aryan Nations encourages the acquisition of arms.

To recruit people, the Aryan Nations has long held a summer festival at Hayden Lake called the World Congress of Aryan Nations. Courses on such things as terrorism and guerrilla warfare are staples at the festival. The Aryan Nations also promotes a prison branch of their organization and publishes a prison outreach newsletter known as the Way.

Familiarity with Nazi sympathizers and other right-wing personalities began early in Butler's life. More than fifty years ago, he joined William Dudley Pelley's Silver Shirts, which was the first National Socialist (Nazi) party in the United States. Beginning in the 1960s, Butler became closely associated with Wesley Swift, who was the founder of the Church of Jesus Christ, Christian, in California. Butler also was the director of the Christian Defense League, an anti-Semitic organization that subscribed to the idea of a Jewish world conspiracy.

During the 1980s, a member of the secret paramilitary terrorist group called the Order used Butler's presses to print counterfeit U.S. currency on the grounds of the Aryan Nations. Butler may also have accepted money that the Order obtained through a series of armed robberies. Whether or not he accepted the money, his ties to the Order are strong. Most members of the Order came from the Aryan Nations, with some from local Klan groups and a neo-Nazi group known as the National Alliance.

Butler was indicted for sedition and conspiracy to overthrow the government in 1988, but he was acquitted.

The entrance to the Aryan Nations headquarters in Hayden Lake, Idaho, displays the group's racist, white-separatist policy.

Sedition is illegal rebellion against government authority. He is still the active leader of the Aryan Nations and communicates regularly with the media. Christian Identity pastor Neumann Britton has been named to take over the Aryan Nations after Butler's death.

One of Butler's long-time associates is neo-Nazi Louis R. Beam, who served in Vietnam as a helicopter door gunner. In the 1960s, he joined a white supremacist group known as the United Klans of America, but by the 1970s, he had left that group to join the Knights of the Ku Klux Klan, where he became associated with far-right presidential candidate David Duke. During the 1980s, Beam led a Klan-connected group known as the Texas Emergency Reserve. One of the Reserve's most flagrant acts was to ride a gunboat near the fishing boats of Vietnamese Americans in the Gulf of

Mexico. The message of the Reserve was clear. They wanted to intimidate the Vietnamese Americans into leaving the area. As the Reserve's boat drew toward the shore, everyone could see how those on board were dressed: in the robes and pointed caps of Ku Klux Klan.

In the 1980s, Beam also became ambassador-at-large for the Aryan Nations. The Nizkor Project,[1] the purpose of which is to keep white supremacists and other far-right spokespeople from denying that the Holocaust took place, has reported that one of Beam's "ambassador" duties was to publish a point system on the Internet for "Aryan Warriors." These "warriors" could win points based on the importance of the public figure or minority group member whom they managed to assassinate.

In 1987, Beam and other leading white supremacists were tried at Fort Smith, Arkansas, on sedition charges. Beam was accused of trying to create civil unrest by planning a series of terrorist acts. There wasn't sufficient evidence to convict him, and he and two others were acquitted. This triumph in the courts increased his image as an invincible hero of the far-right militia movement. By the 1990s, his power in Christian Identity circles was surpassed only by that of Richard Butler.

In 1992, Beam outlined his concept of "leaderless resistance" in his quarterly magazine, the *Seditionist*. The concept was derived partly from the communist model of cells, small units of political activists with leaders who seem unimportant but who are actually connected with a central headquarters. Each cell has no information about what the others are doing, so that if one is caught, the others cannot be exposed. With leaderless resistance, Beam brought the underground concept of the cells one step further. He proposed "phantom cells," an idea he claimed he had borrowed from an anticommunist army colonel as well as the rebels of the American Revolution. Phantom cells have no central headquarters to report to at all. Not only does no cell know what another is doing, but none of them answer to a higher authority. In response to the question of how the cells can possibly cooperate without a central headquarters, Beam answered that they will cooperate instinctively, because all of their members will be such passionate super-patriots that everyone will be of the same mind. Anyone who isn't will have no structure of authority to rely on and will therefore quickly drop out.

Beam's call for leaderless resistance appealed to members of the far-right militias for two reasons. First, it had great practical value. It made complete infiltration of the movement by government informers next to impossible. Second, the idea of leaderless groups matched the psychology of the loners, survivalists, and conspiracy theorists in the movement, most of whom distrusted authority and had gone to great lengths to abolish outside control of their life.

Pastor Pete Peters rose high in the ranks of the Christian Identity movement when he established his Church of Christ in LaPorte, Colorado, in 1977. Peters's sermons often included attacks on Jews, whom he said were a threat to American civilization and were in danger of controlling America. He also claimed that blacks were inferior to whites and that homosexuals should be executed.

Peters's church welcomed members of the Order in the mid-1980s when they were at the height of their criminal activities. The ideas of Peters could also said to be associated with the killing of radio talk-show host Allen Berg. On February 13, 1984, Peters and a colleague were guests on Berg's Denver talk radio program. Berg had an ugly confrontation with them regarding their white supremacist

Talk-show host Allan Berg was murdered by members of the Order four months after an on-air confrontation between Berg and Christian Identity leader Pete Peters.

views. Four months later, Berg was murdered outside his home by several members of the Order who had been infuriated over the confrontation.

During the siege at Ruby Ridge, Peters gave Bo Gritz a letter for Randy Weaver. The letter recommended that Weaver listen to Gritz and do what he said. It expressed the hope that there would be no more bloodshed. It also said that Christian Israelites (members of Christian Identity) were praying for the Weaver family.

If Peters's letter served to soothe Weaver and avoid violence, his subsequent references to the incident on his radio program served to stoke the anger of the far-right militia. Peters compared the death of Weaver's child to the Los Angeles beating of Rodney King by police officers, asking why the national media had given King more coverage. His answer was that the media was controlled by a government conspiracy that strove to put the rights of minorities over those of white people.

Peters's next move after the Ruby Ridge incident was to invite hundreds of ultraconservative speakers, leaders, ministers, and activists to the town of Estes Park, Colorado, to discuss the "injustice and tyranny" of the incident. Many declined, but those who were there heard Louis Beam give the keynote address. Beam warned the people at the conference that the Weavers would not be the last to suffer the persecution of the federal government. He and Peters had devised a new strategy for attracting people to their movement. At the conference, they focused almost exclusively on the illegitimacy and tyranny of the federal government. They left racial and religious issues in the background. Their goal was to attract a wider spectrum of people to their agenda. In many ways, it was successful. After the conference at Estes Park, the movement began growing by leaps and bounds.

Some youthful members of the far-right militia movement have come from the neo-Nazi skinhead groups. These groups first appeared in America in the mid-1980s.[2] Their members were mostly in their teens and twenties and announced their affiliation with shaved heads and tattoos of right-wing images and slogans. They drew their philosophy partly from the working-class skinhead gangs that had arisen slightly earlier in England. Most, though not all, of these groups were violent and racist. They functioned as gangs, sometimes committing bias crimes as a group to show their resentment of nonwhites, gays, or people from higher economic classes. Skinhead cells eventually existed in every region of America, with such names as the National Socialist Skinheads, the Confederate Hammer Skins, Nordic Thunder, and the Legion of Aryan Warriors.

White Aryan Resistance and Aryan Youth Movement founder Tom Metzger poses in 1980 with his publication, the *California Klan News*.

It was Tom Metzger, a former Grand Dragon of David Duke's Ku Klux Klan, who finally lent an organizing hand to the skinheads. Metzger had once belonged to the John Birch Society but had found it and another group called the Minutemen too moderate for his views. He had worked on racist Alabama governor George Wallace's presidential campaign in 1968 and had been ordained as an Identity minister. After running unsuccessfully for office, he founded the White Aryan Resistance (WAR). He produced videotapes to further the cause of white supremacists and even published a revolutionary newspaper for working-class whites.

In 1987, Metzger created a confederation of neo-Nazi skinheads called the Aryan Youth Movement. His son John became its president. Both father and son decided to forgo the skinhead uniform of shaved head, boots, and red suspenders to project a more normal image for the media. Both of them appeared with some of their disciples on TV talk shows and said provocative things that brought them a lot of attention.

The Metzgers' leadership of the skinhead movement was severely damaged when an Ethiopian man, Mulugeta Seraw, was killed by a group of skinheads in Portland, Oregon. A suit brought by the Southern Poverty Law Center and another organization intended to implicate both the Metzgers and the White Aryan Resistance in what had happened. Morris Dees, who was the attorney for the Southern Poverty Law Center, was able to prove that the Metzgers' instructions to the Portland skinheads led to the death of the Ethiopian man. The suit was a success. The Metzgers and WAR were fined millions of dollars. This and other incidents badly weakened the organization. Some remaining skinheads were absorbed into the Christian Identity movement and became members of the Aryan Nations.

Militia Propagandists

While activists spoke, organized, and agitated to enrich the far-right militia movement as a whole, their propaganda experts strove to make information on the militia value system more available. Shortwave radio broadcasts on such stations as the New Orleans–based WRNO, Pennsylvania-based WINB, and Nashville-based WWCR (World Wide Christian Radio) sent antigovernment, anti-Semitic, and pro-gun messages throughout the world. Pamphlets, books, and videos preaching the "one world conspiracy" were advertised in magazines and on the Internet.

One of the militia's most skilled propagandists was Willis Carto. Carto had founded the Washington-based

Liberty Lobby in 1955. It was a group that identified itself as an anticommunist organization interested in patriotic activities and conservative politics. According to the Nizkor Project, however, the actual purpose of the Liberty Lobby was "to rehabilitate Hitlerian National Socialism and agitate on behalf of a neo-Nazi movement in the United States."[3]

By the 1970s, the Liberty Lobby had a blatantly anti-Semitic and racist focus. Its members lobbied against the appointment of Henry Kissinger as secretary of state.[4] They also supported a group of writers known as revisionists, who falsely claim that the Holocaust was a myth and that the gas chambers and death camps of the Hitler regime had never existed. In addition, the Liberty Lobby put out statements supporting the apartheid governments of South Africa and Rhodesia (now Zimbabwe).

Today, Willis Carto's greatest tool for spreading far-right ideas is still the medium of print. His organization distributes a wide selection of extremist political literature dealing with anti-Semitic conspiracy theory and paramilitarism. One of these is a six-hundred-page manifesto called *Imperium*, which was written by Carto's pro-Nazi friend Francis Parker Yockey before he committed suicide in prison. *Imperium* calls for a totalitarian political system based on Hitler's ideas and a revolution based on the "European Revolution of 1933" (Hitler's attempt to take over Europe). Carto is also responsible for the creation of an organization called the Institute for Historical Review, which distributes most of the existing books having to do with the denial of the Holocaust. The Liberty Lobby promotes antigovernment conspiracy-theory ideas through books such as *Black Helicopters over America: Strikeforce for the New World Order*, by Jim Keith. The main idea of the book is that mysterious black helicopters seen in the skies are part of a secret government military force poised to take over the world in the very near future.

The Liberty Lobby's most important publication is a weekly newspaper called the *Spotlight*, which claims to have thousands of readers. The *Spotlight* has published numerous articles presenting conspiracy theories involving the federal government. It prints editorials condemning national gun control and predicting a takeover of the United States by the United Nations. In the January 23, 1995, issue of the *Spotlight*, the headline read: "Arizona Desert May Hold Secret of Foreign Military Equipment for Use Against Americans?"[5] The article suggested that some National Guard helicopters and tanks seen in Arizona were of Russian origin and that the National Guard was being turned into a strike force of the New World Order. According to several government information offices, there are simple explanations for all of this. Russian tanks are on U.S. Army bases because they were brought back from Europe after the end of World War II. And Russian troops have been training on U.S. soil since the end of the Cold War in an attempt to promote better understanding between the two powers. The black helicopters so often referred to by some right-wing militia members actually belong to the National Guard and other agencies and are sometimes used by local law enforcement officers to spot secret marijuana farms.[6] They are not secretly surveying the land in preparation for a surprise takeover.

Many conspiracy theorists, white supremacists, Patriots, and religious rightists use the *Spotlight* to keep in contact with the other factions of their movement. Timothy McVeigh, one of the men convicted of the Oklahoma bombing, once advertised the sale of a military-style antitank launcher in the *Spotlight*. To reach even more people, the

Liberty Lobby also broadcasts two shortwave radio shows, *Radio Free America* and *Editor's Roundtable*, which bring the ideas of the far-right militia movement into the homes of anyone willing to tune them in.

One of the far right's highest-profile media personalities has been Mark Koernke, a University of Michigan janitor who, under the name Mark from Michigan, hosted a nightly shortwave radio program called *Intelligence Report*. Koernke once belonged to the Michigan Militia, but his policies were so militant that he had to form his own militia, which he dubbed the Michigan Militia at Large. Koernke has a criminal record that includes assault and carrying a concealed weapon. On his radio show, Koernke encouraged listeners to become heavily armed, because, he says, the United States is on the brink of being taken over by a secret national police force composed of gangs, Nepalese soldiers, National Guardsmen, and Russian troops just waiting for the signal. Some of Koernke's ideas may have inspired Timothy McVeigh, who was convicted of the Oklahoma City bombing. A cashier at a grocery store in Dexter, Michigan, claimed she saw Koernke with McVeigh and that Koernke and his wife, Nancy, often spoke of Terry Nichols, the other person convicted of the bombing.[7] Koernke denied knowing either McVeigh or Nichols but admitted the possibility that they may have attended a meeting of his Michigan Militia at Large.

In 1995, Koernke went on a speaking tour. A state representative from Pennsylvania, Teresa Brown, actually welcomed him to a high-school auditorium in Meadville, where he spoke for several hours to an audience of a thousand. His message was about the New World Order on our doorstep and how we can avoid the concentration camps supposedly lying in wait for us. Koernke also did a weeklong speaking tour with members of the Militia of Montana, where he promoted his videotapes, which claimed, among other things, that the Environmental Protection Agency was tracking vehicles by remote control, that biochips were being prepared to be inserted into our skin, and that all gun owners would soon be confined to concentration camps.

In 1998, Koernke was accused of beating a process server with his rifle. After a two-month chase, during which Koernke continued to broadcast his shortwave radio show by calling in from secret locations, the police finally caught up with him, and he was arrested. Afterwards, Koernke was also accused of encouraging his radio listeners to shoot Assistant U.S. Attorney Lloyd Meyer, a leading prosecutor of violent people associated with militias.

Perhaps the most influential writer of the far-right militia movement is William L. Pierce, a former college instructor from Oregon with a Ph.D. in physics. In the 1960s, Pierce was assistant to George Lincoln Rockwell, the founder of the American Nazi Party. When Rockwell was killed by a former follower, Pierce joined the National Youth Alliance, a far-right political group. In 1974, he created his own organization, the National Alliance, which is committed to creating an America that is all-white and free of Jews, homosexuals, liberals, and career women.

Under the pen name Andrew Macdonald, Pierce is the author of the notorious book *The Turner Diaries*. This novel is a fantasy, describing a ruthless terrorist war against the federal government and minorities, ending in an all-white fascist American nation of about 50 million people. The *Turner Diaries* contains a passage about the bombing of a federal building. In the novel, this bombing begins the war against the government that finally leads to the new white America. In the novel, the bomb is made by mixing heating oil and ammonium nitrate fertilizer, which is brought to the

The Turner Diaries was written under a pen name by ultra-racist National Alliance founder William Pierce. The novel was used by Timothy McVeigh as a blueprint for his 1995 bombing of the Alfred P. Murrah Federal Building in Oklahoma City.

building in a stolen truck. Both the date and the details of the bombing are remarkably similar to conditions surrounding the actual Oklahoma City bombing. Add this evidence to the fact that the *Turner Diaries* was Timothy McVeigh's favorite book—he often passed out copies at gun fairs—and its use as a blueprint for the worst domestic terrorist attack this country has ever seen becomes glaringly obvious.

Pierce himself has made comments on the radio interpreting the Oklahoma bombing as an unfortunate but necessary step toward a new America. He said he deplored the deaths of innocent people, but he blamed President Clinton and the federal government for what happened. He has stated that conditions in this country justify certain terrorist acts.

In recent years, Pierce has distanced himself from the Christian Identity movement, which he perceives as foolishly religious. He now leads a national organization from his base in West Virginia that rejects traditional religions and focuses on the advancement of the white race. In his second novel, *Hunter*, about a man who assassinates Jews to cleanse the white race, Pierce bashes the members of Christian Identity as country bumpkins who can't convince anyone but hicks to join their movement. This has kept Pierce's National Alliance and the Aryan Nations from forming very close ties.[8]

Leaders of the New Militia

Today's far-right militia groups answer to no central authority. Many of their dealings take place underground. Tensions and disagreements among groups often lead to splintering and new configurations. New groups with new leaders are born regularly. Nevertheless, a few key figures of the movement have become nationally known.

The best-known far-right militia of the 1990s is the Militia of Montana (MOM), founded in 1994 by John Trochmann and his brother David. Some people call it the Mother of Militias. The *Washington Post* referred to Trochmann as the "guru of the American Militia movement." Although he has denied it, Trochmann has been a longtime believer in the philosophy of Christian Identity. He and members of his family have been involved in the most important incidents that shaped the militia movement from the very start. They came to Ruby Ridge to support their friend Randy Weaver during the siege. In 1990, Trochmann was a featured speaker at the Aryan Nations World Congress. In 1992, he went to the Sanders County Courthouse to file a proclamation. In it, he stated, "I am not now, nor have I ever been a citizen of the United States or a resident of its subordinated territories." He was instead, a "free white Christian man" who answered only to the "organic Constitution of the United States."[9] As far as Trochmann is concerned, he is not a citizen of the current government, which is based on a Constitution with twenty-six amendments (some of them naturalizing blacks and foreign-born people). Instead, he subscribes to the original Constitution, which had only ten amendments and no references to blacks or foreigners.

The Militia of Montana's tiny headquarters is in Noxon, Montana, not far from Ruby Ridge. Although the number of official members of the Militia of Montana may only be in the hundreds, thousands more who sympathize with the militia are connected to the office in Noxon by a network of mailings, faxes, phone-calls, talk-radio shows, and the Internet.

Nowadays, Trochmann's group tends to focus less on issues of race and more on issues of gun control and federal intervention. Speaking around the country, Trochmann has terrified thousands of gun owners by the prospect of a coming "gun grab" during which individuals will have to surrender their arms to the federal government. Those people who agree with this first assumption—that their gun rights have been put in jeopardy by the Brady Bill and by a federal ban on assault weapons—are sometimes open to Trochmann's explanation of the larger situation. From him they learn that gun control is merely one step toward the New World Order. They are taught that the United States is about to be conquered by an international conspiracy using weapons and armies of allies scattered throughout the world. They are initiated into the mysteries that associate abortion rights, taxes, public schooling, women's rights, gay rights, and trade treaties with a conspiracy against the ordinary American.

Trochmann's son Randy, a cofounder of the Militia of Montana, sometimes substitutes for his father in important media appearances. After the Oklahoma City bombing, it was he, rather than the gruffer John, who explained to the media that the Militia of Montana thought the bombing had been done by the federal government to draw attention from the investigations into Bill and Hillary Clinton's alleged financial misconduct and from the Brady Bill and to stimulate passage of an antiterrorist bill in Congress. Because Randy looks like a wholesome rodeo star, he often serves as the public relations person for the militia. His father, John, on the other hand, seems to have anger written on his brow. His ample, biblical-looking beard and piercing eyes are a little off-putting to the average TV viewer or newspaper reader.

Members of MOM have been involved in violent encounters with law enforcement, but the group is best known for its speaking tours and publications. One of its books, *The M.O.M. Manual*, is a how-to manual that shows the reader how to sabotage the day-to-day business world and government operations in this country. It offers advice on the kidnapping of media personalities, the execution of spies and government officials, and the spreading of false rumors. Another manual that the organization distributes, called *The Road Back*, gives information on guerrilla warfare and making bombs. MOM also distributes a popular video called "Invasion and Betrayal," which gives a quick overview of the conspiracy theories that obsess far-right militia members. The video contains images of Russian tanks sitting on railroad cars in Montana, Russian chemical warfare materials being loaded into guarded compounds, and Russian weapons waiting to come to this country across the Mexican border.[10]

Norman Olson, cofounder of the Michigan Militia, poses in his gun shop in Alanson, Michigan, in April 1996.

Two other well-known figures of the far-right militia movement are Norman Olson and Ray Southwell, who cofounded the Michigan Militia in 1994. Olson is a Baptist minister and gun-shop owner. Southwell sells real estate and considers himself a patriot. Before he cofounded the Michigan Militia, he had tried to sue his local school board, which he accused of teaching socialist values. Like the Militia of Montana, the Michigan Militia is opposed to gun control and federal law. Soon after the organization was formed, its membership jumped to several thousand. One of its primary focuses is the Second Amendment, which enshrines the right to bear arms. But this militia is also bitterly opposed to the Environmental Protection Agency, which it sees as a conspiracy by the government to grab land from individuals rather than a conservation agency.

From its inception, the Michigan Militia trained twice a month with arms. Its fort was protected by earthworks overlooking steep forested valleys that were several miles from the nearest highway.[11] Olson claimed that thousands of members were ready to travel to Washington in their uniforms, with their weapons, to present the president and Congress with an ultimatum. Until the Oklahoma City bombing, most of the mainstream media did not feel threatened by the existence of the Michigan Militia. A reporter for the *Philadelphia Daily News*[12] described them as follows: "Mostly white males in their 20s and 30s, they wore fatigues and boots and carried semi-automatic assault weapons, including M-16 lookalikes. The guns were unloaded, though, for fear that someone would mistakenly shoot his own foot. They stumbled through an obstacle course, awkwardly practiced bayonet thrusts, and struggled to shimmy across a rope bridge."

Olson, Southwell, and other members of the Michigan Militia appeared on talk shows and the news, clothing their principles in slogans that recalled key moments in American history. On October 24, 1994, United Nations Day, the Michigan Militia demonstrated against the United Nations in Lansing, Michigan, shouting "traitor" at the mayor and scaring officials into removing the United Nations flag from a city parade.

Sometimes, statements from Olson and Southwell seem horribly ill-timed and tasteless. After it was revealed that McVeigh had probably attended Michigan Militia meetings, Olson told a national television audience: "Within two years, I expect to see the Constitution suspended. We will be prepared to defend it."[13] It's true that the Michigan Militia as a group has not been tied to the bombing in any significant way, but such a remark coming at that time was not very reassuring, as it seemed to hint at more violence. Olson later blamed the Oklahoma City bombing on the Japanese government. After many such media faux pas, he was finally asked to resign from his position as leader of the Michigan Militia.

In Phoenix, Arizona, reports of another militia began surfacing after federal agents discovered an arsenal of weapons in a home on a middle-class suburban street. The arsenal included fully automatic machine guns, an adapter for a grenade launcher, seven hundred pounds of the fertilizer ammonium nitrate, which can be used to manufacture explosives, timer fuses, tactical manuals, and other military objects.[14] They arrested a man named Gary Bauer, as well as eleven other people whom they said were coconspirators in a plot to attack some federal buildings, a police headquarters, and a television station. According to the agents, Bauer was the head of the Viper Team, a far-right militia-type group with plans to terrorize Phoenix with a bombing campaign.

On another quiet street in a suburb of Phoenix, agents also raided the house of Dean C. Pleasant and Randy L. Nelson, two Viper Team members who had been far from discreet about their interest in paramilitary activities.[15] According to an article in the *New York Times*, Pleasant had left his grenades in the backyard to dry, after he painted camouflage patterns on them. Nelson slept with his Browning machine gun, named Shirley, attached to the headboard of his bed. Inside the bungalow that the two men shared, agents found grenades, fuses, blasting caps, pistols, machines guns, rifles, and more than 11,000 rounds of ammunition stuffed into closets and dressers.

Most of the members of the Viper Team were blue-collar people, including a doorman, a doughnut baker, a repairman, and a used-furniture salesman. When they were arrested and taken to court, they claimed merely to be weekend warriors who shot cacti in the desert. However, prosecutors characterized them as an urban terror cell. To prove it, they showed the court a video shot by Pleasant, which is a tour of seven local, state, and federal buildings, as well as a television station. It includes instructions to viewers on how to place charges near support columns to collapse the buildings.

In the end, Bauer pleaded guilty to conspiring to use explosives, to teaching others to use them, and to other weapons charges. He faced a harsh possible sentence—on hundred years just for storing ammonium nitrate, a key ingredient in the Oklahoma bomb, in his basement. However, because he pleaded guilty to all eleven counts against him, the sentence was made lighter. Nelson received a five-year, ten-month prison term for conspiracy and weapons possession.[16]

Pleasant was the last to plead guilty to conspiracy and weapons charges. He was sentenced to 712 months in prison. Nevertheless, he stated to the court, "It may seem that if one has impressive weaponry and the skill to use it, that they are a threat. It is my wish that the public understand that Viper Team was defensive in nature."[17] Even after sentencing, the other members of the Viper Team took the same position. They claimed not to have committed any acts of violence or even to have planned them. They were merely readying themselves for self-defense because they felt they were living in dangerous times. For them, accumulating an arsenal large enough for an army and sleeping with weapons posted near their bed was a part of normal, everyday life.

One of the more bizarre standoffs of the 1990s involving the militia occurred at a remote compound in West Texas. On April 27, 1997, three members of a separatist group called the Republic of Texas shot their way into the home of Joe and

Margaret Ann Rowe, wounding Joe Rowe in the shoulder. The couple headed an area home owner's association, but the militia members believed they were federal "moles." The term "moles" refers to spies used by one government to infiltrate another. Acting on false news that an Alpine, Texas, sheriff had killed a Republic of Texas member, the trio had been ordered by Republic of Texas leader Richard McClaren to kidnap the couple as revenge.

The Republic of Texas had attracted national attention in 1996 when its president John C. Van Kirk was photographed at the Alamo and on the steps of the state capitol proclaiming Texas a free nation. He said that the annexation of Texas as a state in 1845 had been illegal and that it had always been a separate country. He claimed that more than 10,000 people had signed up for citizen identification cards for the new "republic." Then, in March 1996, Van Kirk was deposed, and McClaren became the new leader of the Republic of Texas. He and other Republic leaders told the Internal Revenue Service to leave the state and used their own vigilante court to begin a "suit" against the state, the federal government, the United Nations, and the Catholic Church, which they claimed had plundered Texas.

The kidnappers from the Republic of Texas held the Rowes for over a week before releasing them. During the siege, three hundred state troopers and Texas Rangers sought to arrest those responsible. During the final moments, one militia member was killed as he tried to flee. McClaren and his top lieutenant, Robert Otto, were convicted of plotting to kidnap the Rowes. Then McLaren, his wife, and six followers were charged with another crime: issuing more than $1.8 billion of worthless checks in the name of the bogus Republic of Texas, which they used to pay bills.

Angels of Vengeance

Martha A. Bethel's life was nearly ruined by the Militia of Montana.[18] She is a municipal judge in a Hamilton, Montana, court. In January 1995, a man who identified himself as part of the militia movement appeared before her in court for three traffic tickets. He refused to cooperate because he said he was not subject to the laws of Montana. A couple of months later, the man served Judge Bethel with papers claiming that she had violated one of the laws of the "common-law" court he subscribed to, which was called the "Ravalli County Court, Common Law Venue, Supreme Court, Country of Montana." The so-called court was one of several set up by Patriots. The papers the man served demanded that Judge Bethel dismiss the charges against him or she would be arrested.

Bethel later received kidnapping threats from people who accused her of committing treason. She was followed home and harassed by calls. After testifying before the Montana legislature on a bill that would make it a felony to impersonate or harass a public official, she began receiving more threats and hate mail. Eventually, she was informed by a federal law-enforcement agency that there was a contract out for her murder. The police suggested she leave the county and, in the meantime, helped her decide which room of her house would be the safest if it was subjected to gunfire.

To date, Bethel is still alive, but other people who have had confrontations with right-wing extremist organizations have not been so lucky. At least two have met death at the hands of the notorious domestic terrorist group known as the Order. Robert J. Matthews founded the Order in 1983, after working as a recruiter for the National Alliance. The Order was inspired by Pierce's novel *The Turner Diaries* and copied some of its terrorist acts from that piece of fiction. One of the group's most horrendous acts was the murder of Alan Berg, the radio personality who had dared to criticize their activities. Order members also assassinated one of their own, Walter West. In 1984, they decided that he was a threat to their secrecy and security. They drove him into the Idaho wilderness, bludgeoned him with a hammer, shot him, and buried him.

After Order member Thomas Martinez agreed to become a government informer, the FBI began building a case against the organization. By that time the group was responsible for several armed robberies, the bombing of a Seattle theater and a Boise, Idaho, synagogue, and counterfeiting money and passing it. Mathews had escaped to Whidbey Island in the state of Washington, but law enforcement officers caught up with him there in 1984. After a standoff that lasted a day and a half, he was killed when the ammunition he had barricaded himself behind exploded.

In 1987, a white supremacist named Richard Wayne Snell was convicted of killing two people in Arkansas: a black state trooper and a pawnbroker whom he erroneously identified as Jewish. Snell was sentenced to death. In 1995, the Militia of Montana tried to stop Snell's execution by asking its readers to write to the governor of Arkansas. The execution was scheduled for April 19, 1995, the second anniversary of the fire that consumed the Branch Davidian compound in Waco. Snell was executed on April 19, but not until he had seen early television coverage of the bombing of the federal building in Oklahoma City on that same day. Strangest of all was the fact that a person who had testified against Snell had mentioned a plot to bomb the federal building in Oklahoma City and had said he had actually cased that building because Snell had suggested he do it.

Snell's comment to the governor about the bombing, which occurred just before his death, was: "Look over your shoulder. Justice is coming."[19]

BRUTE FORCE: HOW THE MILITIA MOVEMENT FINALLY SHOOK THE WORLD

Richard Wayne Snell's comment to the governor had an irony he never lived to realize. Justice did come, but it came for the militia movement. A few days after the Alfred P. Murrah Federal Building was bombed, there wasn't a single American who hadn't heard of the far-right militias. The bombing branded the far-right Patriot movement with a lasting image of barbarism and infamy. At the same time, it gave many formerly obscure spokespeople for the militia movement a national platform. Some of these people did everything in their power to recast the Oklahoma bombing as a confirmation of their theories. Others used every means to distance the militia movement from what had happened.

The Bombing

The bomb that ripped apart the Alfred P. Murrah Federal Building at 9:02 A.M. on April 19, 1995,[1] left behind an enormous crater of rubble and 168 corpses. More than 500 others were injured. The blast was so powerful that it destroyed several nearby buildings. For two days, rescue workers labored frantically to locate any survivors who might still be trapped in the rubble. The event devastated Americans and left authorities with a long list of unan-

The bombing of the Murrah building in Oklahoma City was the
worst act of domestic terrorism the United States has ever faced.

Survivors of the bombing
are treated by medical teams
after they were evacuated
from the blasted structure.

swered questions. Was it the act of Islamic terrorists similar to those who had bombed the World Trade Center? How many bombs had actually exploded? What kind of bombs were they? Within the first few hours of the bombing, the police, the U.S. Army, and the FBI had collected samples of the rubble in order to isolate traces of the chemical that had exploded. Meanwhile, calls claiming responsibility for the bombing came one after the other. Seeking to capitalize on the panic caused by the incidents, anonymous callers made bomb threats in more than a dozen cities. But the FBI had already found a key piece of evidence. A truck axle bearing a telltale vehicle identification number had been found a couple of blocks from the site of the bombing. The truck had been rented from Elliott's Body Shop in Junction City, Kansas. The people who worked at the shop provided the first descriptions of the suspects. These descriptions resulted in sketches of two subjects, which were released under the names "John Doe No. 1" and "John Doe No. 2."

A little more than an hour after the bombing, Timothy McVeigh was stopped on Interstate 35 near Perry, Oklahoma, because his car was missing a license plate. As soon as the officer got near the car, he noticed that McVeigh had a suspicious bulge in his jacket. The officer discovered that the bulge was caused by a 9-mm Glock semiautomatic. McVeigh was carrying a 6-inch knife as well. Although McVeigh claimed to be driving cross-country, he had no luggage. The officer arrested McVeigh on several misdemeanors, which included carrying a concealed weapon and driving without a license plate. He took him to jail.

McVeigh was supposed to be released the next day because he stated that he could obtain bail. But because of other court business, the arraignment was postponed. Meanwhile, a coworker of McVeigh's who thought he

Timothy McVeigh is moved from Perry, Oklahoma, to Oklahoma City after FBI agents a coworker identified McVeigh in a sketch of the bombing suspects.

recognized one of the John Doe sketches had contacted the FBI. He told the FBI that McVeigh's politics were militant and far to the right and that McVeigh was obsessed with the incident involving the Branch Davidians at Waco. When the FBI ran a computer check of McVeigh's social security number, they located him at the county jail. McVeigh was booked on suspicion of blowing up the Murrah building. He barely reacted, giving only his name, military rank, and date of birth.

At the hearing that followed, evidence linking McVeigh to the explosion accumulated. Someone had seen a person resembling him enter the Murrah building right before the explosion. Another person had information about McVeigh and a man named Nichols on whose family's farm the two men had reportedly been making bombs from fertilizer. During the entire hearing, McVeigh maintained his poker face and offered no information. Afterward he was taken in an armed convoy to the El Reno Federal Correctional Center.

Portrait of Two Terrorists

What kind of a man could retain such apparent composure in the face of such a grave charge? Who were his associates and what common psychology brought them together?

McVeigh was born on April 23, 1968, in Pendleton, a town in Upstate New York. From a young age, he had a fascination with guns. In one of his early jobs as a security guard, he came to work carrying several firearms, with a ribbon of ammunition strung across his chest. His coworkers found this extremely eccentric. His neighbors in a rural part of New York complained to state troopers about his continually disturbing the peace on land he and a friend had purchased for target practice. In 1988, at twenty, he decided to leave civilian life and go to a place where guns were an essential part of everyday life. McVeigh joined the army and was shipped to Fort Benning, Georgia, for basic training. There he met Terry Nichols, who immediately became a close friend.

Terry Nichols was thirty-three years old when he joined the army. Being a soldier was the most recent in a series of unsuccessful occupations, which had included selling real estate, running a grain elevator, and working on his brother's farm. Nichols and McVeigh hit it off immediately, but a year later Nichols left the military. The next year he went to the Philippines hoping to find a wife.

By that time McVeigh was in the infantry at Fort Riley, Kansas. As an armored-tank gunner, he proved his knack for cold-blooded marksmanship. McVeigh was a meticulous, highly disciplined soldier and was promoted to sergeant by the fall of 1990.

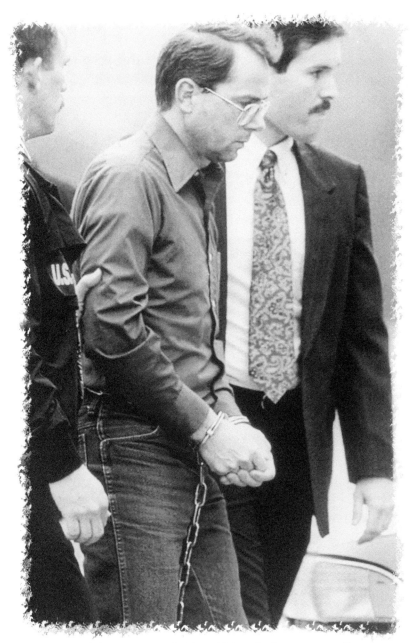

Convicted domestic terrorist Terry Nichols had many connections with the Patriot and militia movements.

As McVeigh made strides in the army, civilian Terry Nichols was involved in a lot of paperwork with the government. He'd found a seventeen-year-old bride in the Philippines and married her, but once he got back home, it took seven months of red tape to bring her to the United States. When she arrived, she was pregnant by her old boyfriend. Nichols vowed to treat the baby as his own, but the child died about two years later. The whole experience infuriated Nichols, who apparently blamed the government delays for his situation.

Meanwhile, in the army, Sergeant McVeigh was developing a reputation for being a racist. He did not fraternize with the African-American soldiers in his unit, and as a supervisor he seemed to reserve the worst grunt work for blacks, regardless of their qualifications. In 1991, McVeigh's unit was sent to the Persian Gulf for Operation Desert Storm, where he was involved in extensive combat. There he proved his prowess as a gunman once again, becoming heady with excitement whenever he accomplished a direct hit in battle, despite the rather gruesome results.

When McVeigh came back to the United States in the spring, he decided to become a Green Beret. But the training at Fort Bragg was too strenuous even for him. He quit after having a hard time meeting the physical requirements for marches. Given McVeigh's mental makeup—his great dependence upon military accomplishment to boost his self-esteem—failing as a Green Beret must have been hard for him to bear. McVeigh had always been attracted to far-right paramilitary politics. He was an avid reader of *Soldier of Fortune* magazine, a favorite of paramilitary enthusiasts. However, after the Green Beret incident, he seemed to become more radical. He became a fanatic gun collector and a promoter of conspiracy theories. He even claimed that the army had once inserted a computer chip into his buttocks so that they could monitor his actions.

Near the end of 1991, McVeigh left the army and joined the National Guard. By that time, he had attended meetings of more than one right-wing militia group. He also wrote letters to a local paper revealing himself as an political extremist who thought the United States might be heading toward civil war.

McVeigh and Nichols hooked up again in the summer of 1992. They spent some time together on the Michigan farm of Nichols's brother James. During the Branch Davidian siege in 1993, McVeigh visited Waco. The spectacle of Waco seemed to put the finishing touches on McVeigh's far-right radicalism. By June of that year, he had moved to Arizona, where he found work through Michael Fortier, a friend from the army with connections to the Arizona Patriots, a far-right paramilitary group. McVeigh began listening to short-wave radio broadcasts of the far right, including those by Mark Koernke. He was a reader of the *Spotlight* and even advertised for sale an antitank missile launcher in its pages under another name. He also went to gun shows, where he handed out copies of his favorite book, The *Turner Diaries*. Wherever he went, McVeigh preached his personal gospel, a diatribe of resentment against the federal government and the one-world conspiracy and a hymn of martyrdom for the Branch Davidians.

McVeigh also visited his friend Terry Nichols in Michigan a few times and reportedly attended at least one meeting of the Michigan Militia. Later, police would trace a phone call he made to an unknown person in Elohim City, a Christian Identity compound on the Oklahoma-Arkansas border.

While McVeigh was developing as a far-right radical, Nichols was filing Patriot-style court papers. He had accumulated a credit card debt of almost $20,000, for which he was sued by two banks. Nichols's defense was that he was not liable for the debt because he was not a citizen of the current corrupt government. He claimed to have paid his debt with a type of check used as currency by some militia and Patriot organizations. The check was worthless, however, within the legitimate American monetary system.

Nichols had other financial problems as well. He owed child support. He gave a similar excuse for not paying: He wasn't a citizen and wasn't subject to the state's jurisdiction. He also destroyed his driver's license, voter registration card, and passport and, like McVeigh, drove without official license plates.

According to court evidence, McVeigh and the Nichols brothers formed a paramilitary cell when McVeigh came for another visit in the spring of 1993. They made bombs on James Nichols's farm and trained for combat. The three were developing a militia mentality so radical that they no longer fit in with most of the established militia organizations.

The Trial

Three weeks after the bombing, McVeigh was still the only suspect charged in the case. Nichols had surrendered just two days after the bombing after hearing that authorities were looking for him.. But he was not charged with the crime until May 10, 1995. The next month, on June 14, authorities acknowledged that John Doe No. 2 was a sketch of an innocent Army private stationed at Fort Riley.

On August 11, a grand jury indicted both McVeigh and Nichols on murder and conspiracy charges. In October,

Attorney General Janet Reno authorized prosecutors to seek the death penalty. In February 1996, Judge Richard Matsch moved the trial to Denver, saying that the media had made it impossible for Nichols and McVeigh to get a fair trial in Oklahoma City. The judge also ruled that McVeigh and Nichols would be tried separately. In consideration of the many people who had lost family and friends in the bombing, he ordered that the trial be shown on closed-circuit television at a government auditorium in Oklahoma City.

Meanwhile, a host of theories about the bombing were circulating, some of them promoted by the far-right militia, others the brainstorms of political analysts or average citizens. Some people claimed that there had to have been at least two explosions, backing their theories up with reports from some University of Oklahoma seismologists.[2] Others suggested that the bomb or bombs were actually planted by someone working for the government, perhaps McVeigh himself. The usual New World Order conspiracy theories reverberated across the airwaves. The public waited tensely for more evidence. Then, in September 1996, the U.S. Geological Survey published a report about the seismic waves recorded during the bombing, which showed beyond a shadow of a doubt that there had only been one explosion.[3]

In April 1996, the taciturn McVeigh released statements to a British newspaper.[4] "For a long time, I thought it was best not to talk about my political views," he said. "But millions share them, and I believe it is gravely wrong that I should allow the government to try and crucify me just for believing what I do." He said that his views were closest to the Patriot movement and called the U.S. government "the omnipresent leader." The statements convinced most Americans that McVeigh had strong ties to the far-right militia, though little evidence actually linking him to it had turned up.

It wasn't until the end of March 1997 that jury selection for McVeigh's trial begin. A couple of weeks before, sensational news about McVeigh flunking a lie detector test had been leaked to the media. *Newsweek* reported[5] that the lie detector test had resulted in McVeigh admitting responsibility for the bombing to his lawyers. It also suggested that McVeigh had given some signals that there were other coconspirators besides Nichols involved in the bombing. These claims were later attacked by other sources as a hoax, but the specter of undiscovered coconspirators loomed throughout the entire trial, never to be disproved.

As the trial drew closer, spokespeople for the far-right militias jockeyed for the best public position on the affair. To condone the act of terrorism would cast them as heartless villains. But they wanted to use the event as a parable about what was wrong with America. Most spokespeople stuck with the assertion that the explosion had been the result of a government conspiracy, an attempt on the part of the government to cast aspersions on the far right. Some said McVeigh was a sacrificial lamb in a government plot. Others said that if McVeigh was indeed the culprit, he had acted out of desperation in the face of a ruthless, autocratic federal government. A very few even went so far as to praise McVeigh. "I think he's a courageous man," said Dennis Mahon, leader of the Tulsa chapter of the White Aryan Resistance. "If we had a hundred men like him in this country we'd probably change things around." Then Mahon tried to soften this brazen statement by adding, "I don't agree with what he did particularly. My personal opinion is that that building should have been bombed early in the morning [meaning before people arrived]."[6]

Before the trial began, the prosecution had assembled a three-pronged body of material evidence, circumstantial evidence, and witness testimony. As material evidence, they had the axle identifying the truck that had been used to carry the bomb. From the wreckage they claimed they had been able to identify the exact nature of the explosive device. They also had McVeigh's fingerprints on a receipt for the bomb material as well as some bomb detonators from Nichols's home. The circumstantial evidence they had did not itself prove guilt, but it wove a web around McVeigh, making it more likely that he was the culprit. This evidence included McVeigh's past experience with explosives, reports of his associations with antigovernment far-right radicals, remarks he had made about his rage over the Branch Davidian incident, and reports about his whereabouts on the days just before the bombing.

Central to the witness testimony was McVeigh's friend Michael Fortier. Fortier admitted that he'd known about the bombing in advance and that he and McVeigh had cased out the Alfred P. Murrah Federal Building. McVeigh's sister, Jennifer McVeigh, was also questioned in an attempt to establish McVeigh's far-right, paramilitary mentality. As it turned out, she had been converted to McVeigh's ideas. Although she claimed to deeply love her brother, her testimony completed the process of defining him as a paramilitary fanatic with deluded, potentially violent political views.

McVeigh's defense team had less going for them. They had to rely on the fact that no one alive had actually seen McVeigh set off the bomb. They also hoped to shed doubt on the expertise of the FBI laboratory and its claims of having found traces of the explosives in places that implicated McVeigh. They planned to attack the character of Michael Fortier, the prosecution's star witness, in an attempt to discredit his testimony.

Another possible defense was to focus on the size of the bomb, which explosive experts claimed was an ammonium nitrate bomb of about five thousand pounds. A bomb of that size, the defense would say, could not have been made by only two men in the time period that was specified by prosecutors. As a long shot, the defense also wanted to suggest that McVeigh was merely a pawn in a complicated international conspiracy involving Iraq, the Irish Republican Army, and some white supremacists. But this last defense was never allowed.

As the trial progressed, the evidence against McVeigh became crushing. Prosecutors painted a picture of a sinister change in mentality on McVeigh's part with letters he had written claiming that his thoughts had shifted from the "intellectual . . . to the animal" and that "something big" was about to happen.[7] They maintained that McVeigh had spent months planning the bombing. To back up that claim, they put Fortier and his wife on the stand, where both talked about how McVeigh had diagrammed the construction of the Murrah building on their kitchen floor and used soup cans to demonstrate how he planned to blow it up. The prosecutors also claimed that McVeigh and Nichols had used aliases to purchase the ammonium nitrate fertilizer and that McVeigh had gone on a nationwide search to find some of the other ingredients in the bomb. Throughout the disposition of all this evidence, the prosecutors wove an emotional narrative of the day of the bombing, which they hoped would stir the feelings of jurors.

On May 21, the prosecutors rested their case. There were still some holes in it. No witness could place McVeigh in Oklahoma City on the day of the explosion. None of McVeigh's fingerprints had been found on the rental contract for the truck, in the truck rental office, or on the storage lockers in which the prosecutors said McVeigh kept the explosives. Nevertheless, Assistant U.S. Attorney Larry Mackey wrapped things up with a stirring closing argument:

> Tim McVeigh is a domestic terrorist. But he didn't start that way. The bombing that took place on April 19 in downtown Oklahoma City didn't happen overnight. . . . And you have learned from words written by Tim McVeigh exactly when he stepped over the line, when he formed that specific intent, and when that evolution to terrorism had finished its course.
>
> He told people of his intent to kill long before he killed. The event that may have triggered Tim McVeigh to do the bombing is not clear. But one thing that is clear . . . is that Tim McVeigh had six solid months to abandon that intent, six solid months to think about it, think about it again, and walk away. And instead he drove to Oklahoma City with the truck bomb.
>
> Make no mistake about it: In America, everybody has a right to their beliefs, has a right to think and say what they do. This is not a prosecution of Tim McVeigh for his political beliefs. This is a prosecution of Tim McVeigh because of what he did: He committed murder. This is a murder case.[8]

A happy Denver resident holds up a local newspaper displaying the bombing-trial verdict.

On June 2, 1997, after 23½ hours of deliberation, the jury convicted McVeigh on all eleven counts of murder and conspiracy. When it came time for the jury to decide the sentencing, the judge barred certain emotional material that the prosecution wanted to present, including wedding photographs and poems written by relatives and friends of the victims.[9] McVeigh's lawyers made their last appeal to the jury by explaining his rage over the Branch Davidian incident and his descent into the tangled conspiratorial mentality of the militia movement. His parents pleaded for his life and shared their memories of what they termed his happy childhood. Nevertheless, he was sentenced to death by the jury. His response to the sentencing with short and cryptic. He read a quotation from a 1928 opinion by Supreme Court Justice Louis Brandeis that stated, "Our government is the omnipotent, the omnipresent teacher. For good or ill, it teaches the whole people by its example." Today McVeigh waits on death row and might appeal the verdict.

Terry Nichols's trial began on November 3, 1997. During it some disturbing evidence that has never been explained surfaced. A witness named Charles Farley testified that he had seen not two, but a group of men, standing around a truck that fit the description of the one used for the bombing. Other witnesses said they had seen McVeigh with other men, whom the press suggested might be undiscovered co-conspirators in the bombing.[10]

On December 23, 1997, Nichols was convicted of conspiracy and involuntary manslaughter, but he was acquitted of weapons and explosives charges. In January, the jury came to a deadlock about his sentencing, and Nichols escaped the death penalty. The judge sentenced Nichols to life without parole.

BRUSH FIRES:
THE CONTINUING DRAMA
OF THE MILITIAS

The trials of Timothy McVeigh and Terry Nichols cast a lasting pall over the nation. For the first time, everyone was talking about the far-right militia movement. Up until the bombing, the phenomenon had seemed remote and ridiculous to the average American. Suddenly, it seemed terrifyingly near. The most frightening thing about it was how much damage small groups—or even individual terrorists—could do. At the same time, some people hoped that the movement had been discredited by the tragic outcome of the Oklahoma City bombing, as well as by the portrait of McVeigh that had emerged from the trial. Unfortunately, those hopeful people seem to have been wrong. As late as 1998, the far-right Patriot movement seemed to be expanding, although the number of militias was decreasing. Patriot-inspired crimes flared up like small brush fires throughout the nation. Thankfully, none of the incidents came close to the devastation of the Oklahoma City bombing. Even so, new trends in paramilitary terrorism, such as germ warfare, seemed to be emerging. So were new ideological emphases.

Militias and Antiabortionists

In 1998, one new ideological trend seemed to be a growing link between the antiabortion movement and the far-right

102

militia movement. For decades a far-right fringe had been included in the larger movement opposing abortion. But new connections between this group and the paramilitary movement began forming in the 1990s. On January 29, 1998, an abortion clinic in Birmingham, Alabama, was bombed, causing the death of one police officer and the wounding of a clinic worker. The suspect in the bombing, Eric Rudolph, was a white supremacist with connections to a Christian Identity group known as the Northpoint Tactical Teams.

The search for Rudolph led to a remote area of the Great Smoky Mountains in North Carolina. This area had several small communities, all of which were nearly 100 percent white. According to the Southern Poverty Law Center,[1] these remote hillsides were the training grounds of several far-right groups. As of late 1999, Rudolph had not been found, despite the efforts of a team of up to two hundred agents using sophisticated tracking devices, such as night-vision goggles and heat sensors. Even James "Bo" Gritz, the militia leader who mediated in the Ruby Ridge incident and came to aid the search with a team of more than sixty people, couldn't locate Rudolph. It soon became obvious that one reason was that many of Rudolph's neighbors had no intention of turning him in. Theirs was a small rural community with tight bonds. Although they may not have approved of the act that Rudolph was accused of, their loyalty to him and their suspicion of the government made them keep their mouths shut.

According to the Southern Poverty Law Center, the Rudolph incident was a disturbing sign of a new coalition between right-wing antiabortion ideologues and paramilitary groups. This is happening partly because the stigma of the Oklahoma bombing has prompted the far-right militias to look for more popular social issues with which to identify.

Isolated Acts

Recent events involving the far right have highlighted the fact that danger is coming less and less from organized movements. If members of the militia movement can create havoc in this country, it will not happen through the mass armies of vengeance that they envision. Instead, it will come from a growing number of extremists acting alone or in small groups. The Republic of Texas is proof of such a trend. Its members share the belief that the state of Texas is really an independent nation. Their activism on behalf of this idea is often expressed through individual deeds.

In 1998, several clashes with authorities involved people purported to be members of the Republic of Texas militia. First, five members were indicted in a conspiracy and mail-fraud case. On the date of their hearing, January 14, none of them showed up. Just two weeks later, another Republic of Texas member named Carol Davis Walker was sentenced to ten years in prison for having burned down her own home. The arson was an attempt to collect insurance money on the house. The judge in charge of the case decided to revoke Davis's right to probation based on charges of criminal conspiracy to commit capital murder that related to an attack ten years before on Davis's sister's husband. The next month, the "secretary of state" and Web programmer of the Republic of Texas pleaded guilty to income tax evasion and agreed to cooperate in paying approximately $13,000 in back taxes.

One of the most bizarre crimes of 1998 to come out of the Republic of Texas was an attempt by three men to assassinate President Clinton and other government officials with a deadly toxin. Johnnie Wise, Jack Abbott Grebe Jr., and Oliver Dean Emigh were convicted of conspiracy to use weapons of mass destruction after it was discovered they allegedly were developing a weapon made of a cactus thorn tipped with anthrax, botulism, or the AIDS virus. They had planned to adapt a cigarette lighter to expel air rather than propane so that it could be used to fire the thorn. Their targets were President Clinton, Attorney General Janet Reno, FBI Director Louis Freeh, and other government officials.

Another bizarre event in 1998 involved the threat of chemical terrorism. On February 19, 1998, William Leavitt and Larry Harris were arrested and jailed on charges of possession of anthrax bacteria. Harris is a microbiologist. He is also a white supremacist and a former member of the Aryan Nations. According to a criminal complaint, he had revealed plans several months before to release the bacteria in the New York subway system.

Anthrax is one of the oldest known diseases. It used to be epidemic in many parts of the world but now appears only infrequently in the United States. Animals can catch the disease by drinking contaminated water. Humans can catch it by handling infected materials or by inhaling the spores of the bacterium. The mortality rate for humans is about 20 percent.

An informant told the FBI that Harris and Leavitt, who owns microbiology labs in Nevada and Germany, approached him to test some bacteria and then offered to buy his testing equipment for a huge sum of money. The informant was cooperating with the FBI, so that when the three men met to close the deal, Leavitt and Harris were arrested. In their car were leather flight bags that had been marked with the word "biological." In the end, the substance turned out not to be anthrax bacteria, but anthrax vaccine, which is harmless. The serious charges against the two men were dropped, but that didn't alleviate all of the authorities' anxiety. They knew that Harris had been traveling the far-right

Larry Wayne Harris may be one of a new breed of domestic terrorists. He was convicted of illegal possession of bubonic plague germs and writes extensively on germ warfare.

militia circuit, lecturing on anthrax and other biological weapons. He has written booklets and made videos—all advertised on the Web—that explain how to make or defend against such toxins as bubonic plague and anthrax.

When the anthrax scare turned out to be bogus, people who had been following the story sighed with relief. However, experts in domestic and international terrorism pointed out that there has been increasing interest on the part of terrorists in getting hold of biological weapons. During 1997, the FBI made one hundred criminal investigations into germ warfare. This was a 300 percent increase over the number of such cases the previous year.[2]

Fighting the Threat of the Far-Right Militias

Until the Oklahoma City bombing, federal and state monitoring of unauthorized paramilitary organizations was sketchy and largely ineffective. In 1995, twenty-four states had laws banning private military organizations, and another twenty-four had laws prohibiting private military training if it was likely to produce civil disorder.[3] However, details of these laws varied widely from state to state. Some states had no laws banning unauthorized military groups per se. Others merely required them to register. Still others banned all unauthorized military groups whatever their stated purpose was. Finally, the Brady Bill had toughened the requirements of gun ownership. But despite all of these laws, far-right militia involvement continued to increase throughout the 1990s.

After the Oklahoma bombing, several versions of a new federal antiterrorist bill were discussed in Congress. Positions on the bill wavered. Most representatives thought that there was a need for stronger monitoring, control, and punishment of illegal paramilitary activities. But some also feared giving federal agents too much local power. They also were wary of dispensing with certain legal rights in cases against suspected terrorists.

When the Anti-Terrorism Law of 1996 was finally passed, the provisions it contained relating to domestic terrorism were as follows:[4]

- Creating a federal death penalty for terrorist murders
- Making crimes against a federal employee a federal offense and increasing penalties for these crimes
- Authorizing a study on the possibility of tagging explosives for tracking and identification
- Stiffening penalties for conspiracies involving explosives
- Adding penalties for possession of nuclear material
- Criminalizing the use of chemical weapons
- Asking the attorney general to issue a report on whether bomb-making literature is protected by the First Amendment
- Giving the secretary of state authorization to identify a group as terrorist and forbid it from raising funds; the secretary of state can also freeze the assets of such organizations
- Limiting appeals of state court death-penalty sentences in the federal courts to a one-year period
- Offering restitution to victims of some federal crimes
- Authorizing more than $1 billion over five years for federal, state, and local government programs designed to prevent or deal with terrorists; of these funds, $468 million will go to the FBI for counterterrorism and counterintelligence efforts

Once the bill was passed, some critics on both sides of the issue began calling it ineffective. Some who emphasize individual liberties said that the money awarded to the FBI would bring federal watchdogs into every community, a first step toward a military state. Others said that the provisions were too general and should have been more specifically targeted to identifying and immediately stopping groups known to be engaged in paramilitary activities. However, it's difficult to analyze the actual effects of the law on the militia movement. After its passage, militia violence continued to proliferate throughout the United States, but none of the activities seemed organized on any large scale. This could be partly due to increased pressures on the movement by the new law, which forces militia activity further underground.

Antimilitia Activism

Perhaps a more dynamic way of combating dangerous militias has come from private organizations whose main purpose is monitoring the far right or fighting it in court. Chief among these is the Southern Poverty Law Center in Montgomery, Alabama, which uses three methods to combat hate groups: bringing legal suits against the hate groups in court, monitoring their activities and making people aware of them, and promoting educational efforts to lead to greater tolerance of different races and religions.

Morris Dees is the chief counsel for the Southern Poverty Law Center and its Militia Task Force. The center created the Militia Task Force in October 1994 after its monitoring activities discovered multiple links between white supremacist groups and militias. As part of the Militia Task Force's strategies, Dees has written letters to the attorney general of the United States and to those of several individual states encouraging them to keep a close watch on the militias. The Militia Task Force is also an Internet watchdog, keeping track of Web sites relating to the Patriot movement and militias.

Dees and staff attorney Ellen Bowden are also pushing for states to use existing state laws to shut down dangerous militias. Dees and Bowden say they do not think current antimilitia laws are a violation of free speech and association. The laws do not prevent anyone from speaking out against the government. They also do not prevent people from meeting together as a group—unless they are meeting as a military unit. Dees and Bowden have posted their model Anti-Militia Statute[5] on the Southern Poverty Law Center's Internet site in hopes that it will serve as a guideline for all states in the Union. The statute reads as follows:

A. Any two or more persons who associate as a military organization or demonstrate with arms in public without the governor's authority shall be guilty of a Class _____ misdemeanor.
B. A military organization is any unit with arms, command structure, training and discipline designed to function as a combat support unit.
C. This section does not apply to any school or college where military training and instruction is given under the provisions of state or federal laws.

There are other Internet watchdog groups, legal activism groups, and educational organizations fighting to oppose far-right militias.

The Anti-Defamation League (ADL), founded in 1913, is one of these. It is the world's leading organization in the fight against anti-Semitism. In 1994, it became one of the first organizations to document thoroughly the threat of the

Protesters display signs at a 1991 Klan rally in Denver. Such civil actions may be the best way to fight the activities of such racist and violent organizations.

new far-right militias. In a September 1998 report, the ADL claimed that their research had shown that William Pierce's National Alliance, a neo-Nazi group, was the single most powerful organized hate group in the United States today. According to their report, the National Alliance now has "16 active cells from coast to coast, an estimated membership of 1,000 and several thousand additional Americans listening to its radio broadcasts and browsing its Internet site."[6] Although the ADL's educational and activist programs deal primarily with anti-Semitism, the growing link between anti-Semitism and paramilitary groups has widened its focus to include the militia movement.

Finally, just as there are a growing number of alienated, isolated individuals with a far-right militia mentality, so are there a growing number of individuals without connection to any particular group who want to do something about the danger of the militias. The far-right militia movement deeply offends their values. They may express their antimilitia views by writing to government officials or to newspapers. Or they may be involved in community lobbying efforts to keep the militia mentality out of their schools, community centers, or places of worship. They may be teachers with a good grasp of the real foundations of the American government or clergy with a strong consciousness of the antiviolent, antiracist bases of their religion. Such people may well prove themselves to be the real "army of citizens" when it comes to opposing the militia. In their everyday dealings with neighbors, family, coworkers, and friends, they may be doing more to stem the growing threat of the far-right militia than any organization or government agency can ever achieve.

Notes

Chapter 1

1. From the Southern Poverty Law Center Web site at www.splcenter.org/intelligenceproject
2. Described in Morris Dees with James Corcoran, *Gathering Storm: America's Militia Threat* (New York: HarperCollins, 1996), pp. 14–15.
3. Kenneth S. Stern, *A Force upon the Plain: The American Militia Movement and the Politics of Hate* (Norman: University of Oklahoma Press, 1997), pp. 19–20.
4. Dees, p. 2.
5. John Diamond, "Militias Lure Folks Feeling 'Pushed'" *Philadelphia Daily News,* April 27, 1995, p. 18.
6. Ibid.
7. Mark Fisk, "Teens in the Militia," *Philadelphia Daily News*, May 3, 1995, p. 16.
8. Rogers Worthington, "Far-Right Info. Web: Rumors, Untruths," *Chicago Tribune*, April 26, 1995, Internet version.
9. Dees, p. 6.
10. Stern, pp. 19–20.
11. Stern, pp. 46–47.
12. David H. Bennett, *The Party of Fear: The American Far Right from Nativism to the Militia Movement*, 2nd ed., (New York: Vintage, 1995), p. 2.
13. Bennett, p. 429.
14. Dees, p. 4.

Chapter 2

1. Stern, p. 21.
2. Dees, p. 11.
3. Dees, p. 15.
4. Stern, p. 22.
5. David Johnson, "FBI Exec Admits He Destroyed Ruby Ridge Critique," *Syracuse Herald-Journal*, October 31, 1996, p. A7.

6. Dees, p. 24.

7. Stern, p. 29.

8. Stern, p. 32.

9. Johnson, *Syracuse Herald-Journal.*

10. "The Line at Ruby Ridge," *Miami Herald*, August 17, 1995, p. 20a.

11. Quoted in Victoria Loe, "Wounded Sect Leader, in Rambling Interview, Says That He Is Christ," *Dallas Morning News,* March 1, 1993, Internet version.

12. Quoted in Lee Hancock, "TV Cameraman Admits His Words Tipped Off Cult," *Dallas Morning News*, August 28, 1993, Internet version.

13. Stern, p. 59.

14. Dees, p. 70.

15. Bill Marvel, "Keeping Watch: Gawkers, Profit-seekers, Proselytizers Flock to Hill Near Cult Compound," *Dallas Morning News*, March 16, 1993, Internet version.

16. Lee Hancock, "Deadly Inferno: FBI Says Cult Torched Compound; 26 Believed Dead," *Dallas Morning News*, April 20, 1993, Internet version.

17. Lee Hancock, "Cultists' Lawyers Accuse FBI of Precipitating Violent Ending," *Dallas Morning News*, April 20, 1993, Internet version.

18. Stern, pp. 61–63.

19. Stern, p. 62.

Chapter 3

1. The Nizkor Project maintains a Web site with this information at http://www.nizkor.org/

2. Bennett, pp. 435–436.

3. Nizkor Project Web site.

4. Bennett, pp. 256–357.

5. Quoted in Stern, p. 149.

6. Stern, p. 100.

7. Paul De la Garza and Flynn McRoberts, "Terror in the Heartland," *Chicago Tribune*, April 25, 1995, Internet version.

8. Bennett, pp. 437–438.

9. Stern, p. 69.

10. Bennett, pp. 450–452.

11. Stern, p. 97.

12. "Pair's Tie to Militia Probed; Group's Activism Linked to Waco Raid, 2nd Year Anniversary," *Philadelphia Daily News*, p. 4

13. Bennett, pp. 456–457.

14. V. Dion Haynes and Mike Dorning, "Weapons Cache Found in Militia Suspects' Homes," *Chicago Tribune*, July 3, 1996, Internet version.

15. James Brooke, "Volatile Mix in Viper Militia: Hatred Plus Love for Guns," New York Times, July 5, 1996, electronic library version.

16. Luna I. Shyr, "Viper Militiamen Sentenced," AOLNewsProfiles@aol.net, Associated Press, March 21, 1997.

17. "Viper Militia Man Enters Plea," AOLNewsProfiles@aol.net, Associated Press, March 3, 1997.

18. Martha A. Bethel, "I Received Threats from the Militia of Montana," *New York Times*, July 28, 1995, p. 19A.

19. Stern, p. 57.

Chapter 4

1. Some of the information about the Oklahoma City bombing and the lives of McVeigh and Nichols in this chapter was obtained from Stern's, *A Force upon the Plain*, pp. 179–199.

2. Howard Witt, "Amid Oklahoma Mysteries, Conspiracy Ideas Win Hearing: Threads of Truth Knit Theory Boosted by Former FBI Agent," *Chicago Tribune*, May 9, 1995, Internet version.

3. "Oklahoma Building Seismogram: 1 Bomb," AOLNewsProfiles@aol.net, September 7, 1996.

4. "McVeigh: 'Millions Share My Politics'," *Philadelphia Daily News*, April 22, 1996, p. 23.

5. In Tracy Connor, "McVeigh Failed Lie Test Report," *New York Post*, March 17, 1997, p. 15.

6. James Ridgeway, "Armies of the Right," Village Voice, March 25, 1997, p. 37.

7. "McVeigh Case Highlights," AOL News, Associated Press. May 21, 1997.

8. Excerpts from transcripts of McVeigh trial, furnished by WESTLAW® to AOL News, Associated Press, May 5, 1979.

9. Steven K. Paulson, "Bomb Trial Judge Bars Some Testimony," AOL News, Associated Press, June 13, 1997.

10. James Ridgeway, "Making the Case for a Wider Conspiracy in Oklahoma City," *Village Voice*, December 16, 1997.

Chapter 5

1. Ginger Thompson, "Fugitive Gains Hero Status in Native Region," *Chicago Tribune*, July 17, 1998, Internet version.

2. Vincent J. Schodolski, and V. Dion Haynes, "Toxic Terrorism Threat Is Spreading, Experts Warn," *Chicago Tribune*, February 21, 1998, Internet version.

3. Stern, p. 233.

4. For text of bill, see Legitech Web site at
   www.legiweb.legislate.com/d/s735/s735.txt
5. From the Southern Poverty Law Center Web site:/
   www.splcenter.org/intelligenceproject/ip-6.html
6. "ADL Report Cites Neo-Nazi National Alliance as
   Most Dangerous Organized Hate Group in America,"
   from Anti-Defamation League Web site: www.adl.org/

TO FIND OUT MORE

Anti-Defamation League
823 United Nations Plaza
New York, NY 10017
(212) 490-2525
http://www.adl.org
Monitors extremist movements, especially those that
are anti-Semitic.

Center for Democratic Renewal
P.O. Box 50469
Atlanta, GA 30302
(404) 221-0025
Maintains a database on the far right and publishes
several newsletters.

Coalition For Human Dignity
P.O. Box 40344
Portland, OR 97240
Monitors right-wing activities in the Pacific Northwest.
(503) 281-5823

The Militia Watchdog
http://www.militiawatchdog.org
Internet site devoted to tracking and reporting on
antigovernment extremist activity in the United States.

Montana Human Rights Network
P.O. Box 1222
Helena, MT 59624
(406) 442-5506
Coalition of Montana organizations opposed to hate crimes. Maintains archives.

People for the American Way
2000 M St. NW, Suite 400
Washington, DC 20036
(202) 467-4999
Provides data on media coverage of right-wing activities. Helps other groups resist these movements.

Southern Poverty Law Center
P.O. Box 548
Montgomery, AL 36101
(205) 264-0286
http://www.splcenter.org
The center brings suits against paramilitary and other extremist groups. Publishes the quarterly *Intelligence Report.*

FOR FURTHER READING

Abanes, Richard. *American Militias: Rebellion, Racism and Religion*. Downes Grove, IL.: Intervarsity Press, 1996.

Bennett, David H. The Party of Fear: *The American Far Right from Nativism to the Militia Movement*. New York: Vintage, 1995.

Coppola, Vincent. *Dragons of God: A Journey through Far-Right America*. Atlanta: Longstreet Press, 1997.

Dees, Morris, with James Corcoran. *Gathering Storm: America's Militia Threat*. New York: HarperCollins, 1996.

Dyer, Joel. *Harvest of Rage: Why Oklahoma City Is Only the Beginning*. Boulder, CO.: Westview Press, 1997.

Stern, Kenneth S. *A Force upon the Plain: The American Militia Movement and the Politics of Hate*. Norman: University of Oklahoma Press, 1997.

Wills, Gary. *A Necessary Evil: A History of American Distrust of Government*. New York: Simon and Schuster, 1999.

INDEX